降去神通

AVATAR

THE LAST AIRBENDER™

Created by
Bryan Konietzko
Michael Dante DiMartino

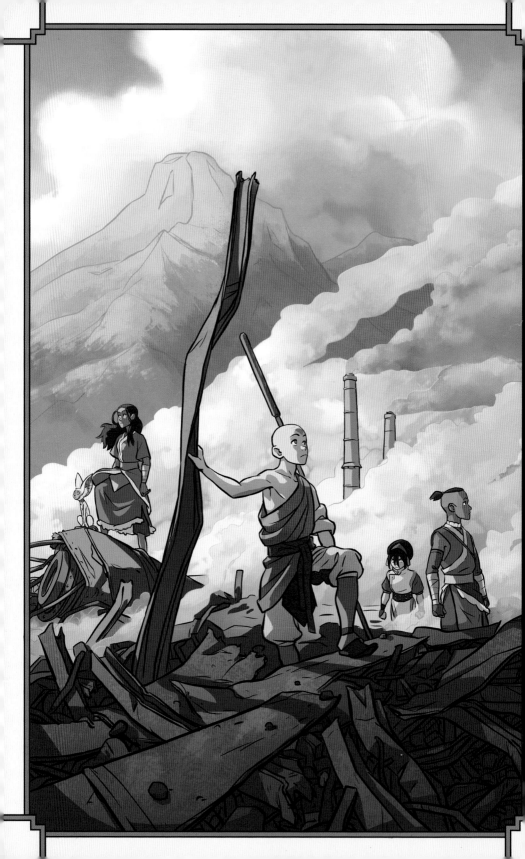

nickelodeon™

降击神通

AVATAR

THE LAST AIRBENDER™

IMBALANCE · PART TWO

script
FAITH ERIN HICKS

art
PETER WARTMAN

colors
ADELE MATERA

lettering
**RICHARD STARKINGS &
COMICRAFT'S JIMMY BETANCOURT**

cover
PETER WARTMAN with **RYAN HILL**

DARK HORSE BOOKS

president and publisher
MIKE RICHARDSON

editors
DAVE MARSHALL and **RACHEL ROBERTS**

assistant editor
JENNY BLENK

collection designer
SARAH TERRY

digital art technician
CHRISTIANNE GILLENARDO-GOUDREAU

martial arts consultant and model
TODD BALTHAZOR

Special thanks to Linda Lee, Kat van Dam, James Salerno, and Joan Hilty
at Nickelodeon, and to Bryan Konietzko and Michael Dante DiMartino.

Published by **Dark Horse Books**
A division of Dark Horse Comics LLC.
10956 SE Main Street, Milwaukie, OR 97222

DarkHorse.com
Nick.com

To find a comics shop in your area, visit comicshoplocator.com

First edition: May 2019 | ISBN 978-1-50670-652-8

1 3 5 7 9 10 8 6 4 2
Printed in China

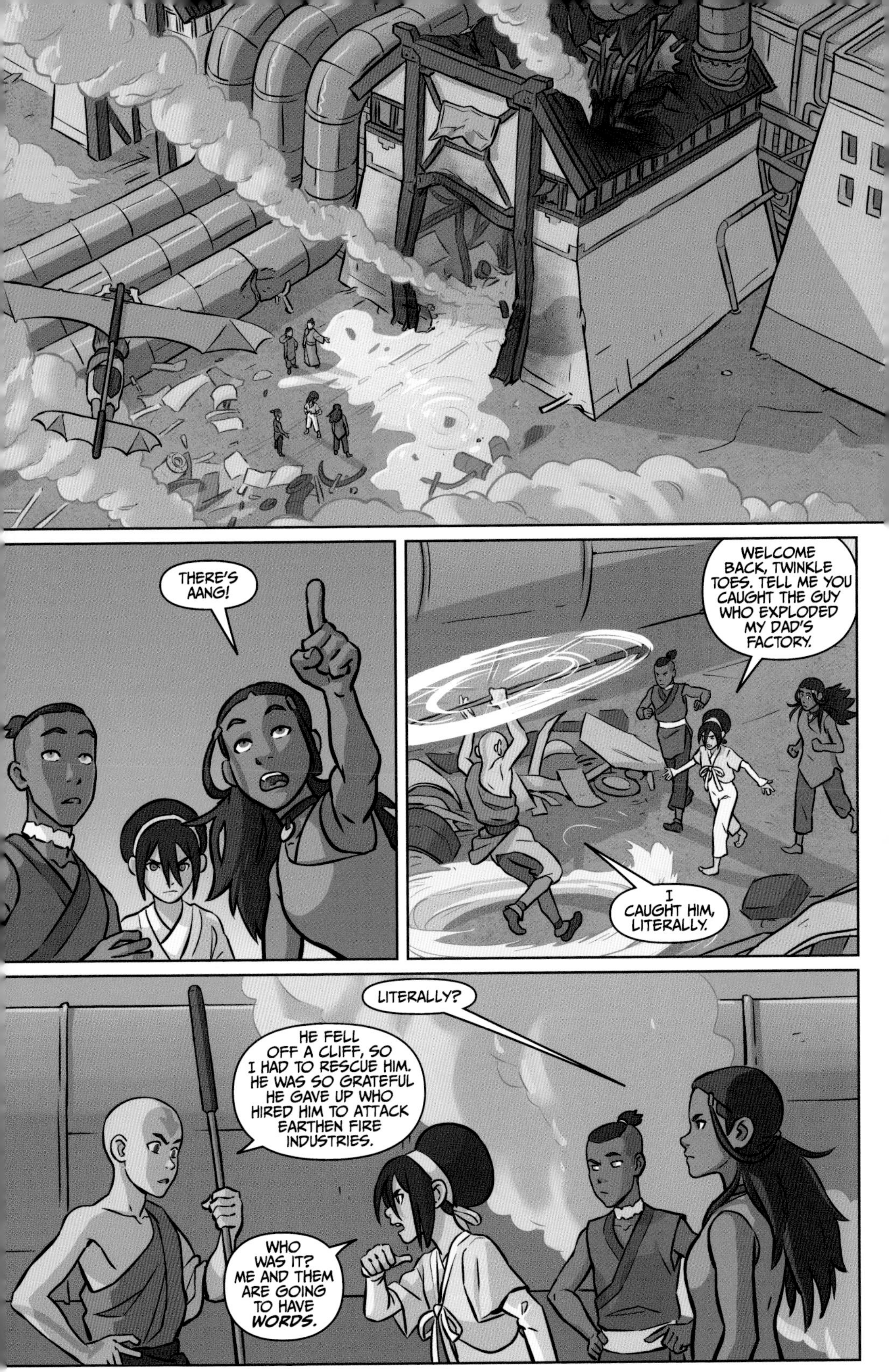
THERE'S AANG!
WELCOME BACK, TWINKLE TOES. TELL ME YOU CAUGHT THE GUY WHO EXPLODED MY DAD'S FACTORY.
I CAUGHT HIM, LITERALLY.
LITERALLY?
HE FELL OFF A CLIFF, SO I HAD TO RESCUE HIM. HE WAS SO GRATEFUL HE GAVE UP WHO HIRED HIM TO ATTACK EARTHEN FIRE INDUSTRIES.
WHO WAS IT? ME AND THEM ARE GOING TO HAVE *WORDS*.

THE FIREBENDER SAID HE WAS HIRED BY TWO TEENAGE GIRLS, ONE OF WHOM WAS A SKILLED EARTHBENDER.

WHY WOULD AN EARTHBENDER HAVE A GRUDGE AGAINST EARTHEN FIRE INDUSTRIES? MY PEOPLE SHOULD KNOW BETTER THAN THAT.

WAS THERE A REASON BEHIND THE ATTACK?

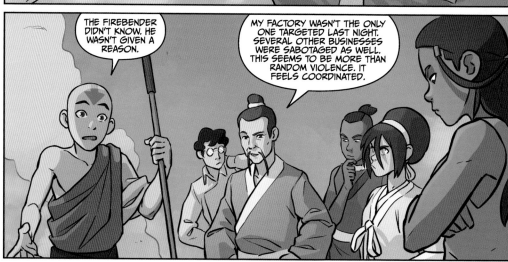

THE FIREBENDER DIDN'T KNOW. HE WASN'T GIVEN A REASON.

MY FACTORY WASN'T THE ONLY ONE TARGETED LAST NIGHT. SEVERAL OTHER BUSINESSES WERE SABOTAGED AS WELL. THIS SEEMS TO BE MORE THAN RANDOM VIOLENCE. IT FEELS COORDINATED.

THERE'S SOMETHING STRANGE GOING ON IN CRANEFISH TOWN. SOMETHING LURKING BENEATH THE SURFACE, LIKE A CATGATOR WAITING TO LEAP OUT AND CLAIM ITS PREY.

TIME FOR TEAM AVATAR INVESTIGATIONS TO DELVE INTO THESE MYSTERIOUS GOINGS-ON!

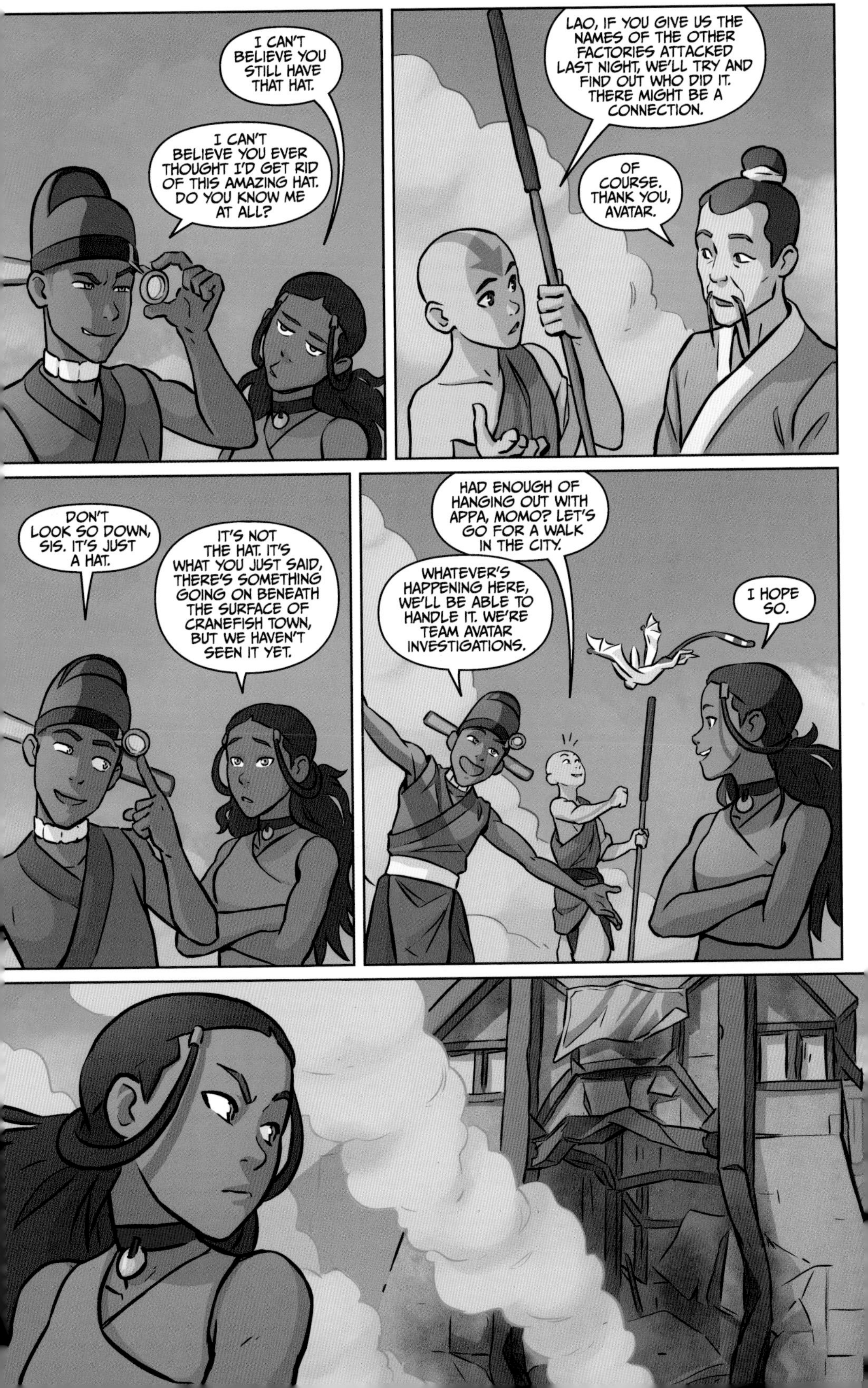
I CAN'T BELIEVE YOU STILL HAVE THAT HAT.
I CAN'T BELIEVE YOU EVER THOUGHT I'D GET RID OF THIS AMAZING HAT. DO YOU KNOW ME AT ALL?
LAO, IF YOU GIVE US THE NAMES OF THE OTHER FACTORIES ATTACKED LAST NIGHT, WE'LL TRY AND FIND OUT WHO DID IT. THERE MIGHT BE A CONNECTION.
OF COURSE. THANK YOU, AVATAR.
DON'T LOOK SO DOWN, SIS. IT'S JUST A HAT.
IT'S NOT THE HAT. IT'S WHAT YOU JUST SAID, THERE'S SOMETHING GOING ON BENEATH THE SURFACE OF CRANEFISH TOWN, BUT WE HAVEN'T SEEN IT YET.
HAD ENOUGH OF HANGING OUT WITH APPA, MOMO? LET'S GO FOR A WALK IN THE CITY.
WHATEVER'S HAPPENING HERE, WE'LL BE ABLE TO HANDLE IT. WE'RE TEAM AVATAR INVESTIGATIONS.
I HOPE SO.

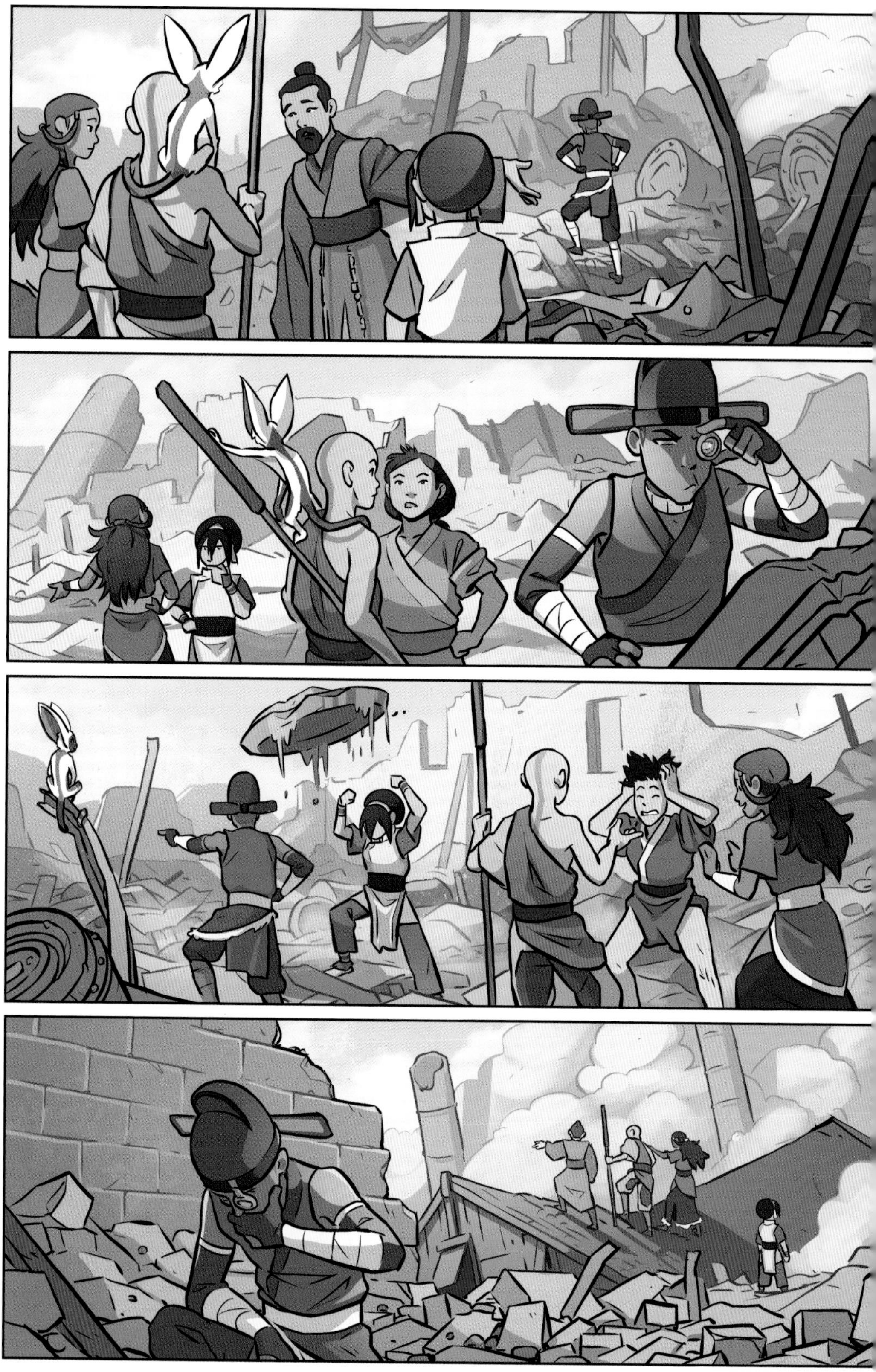

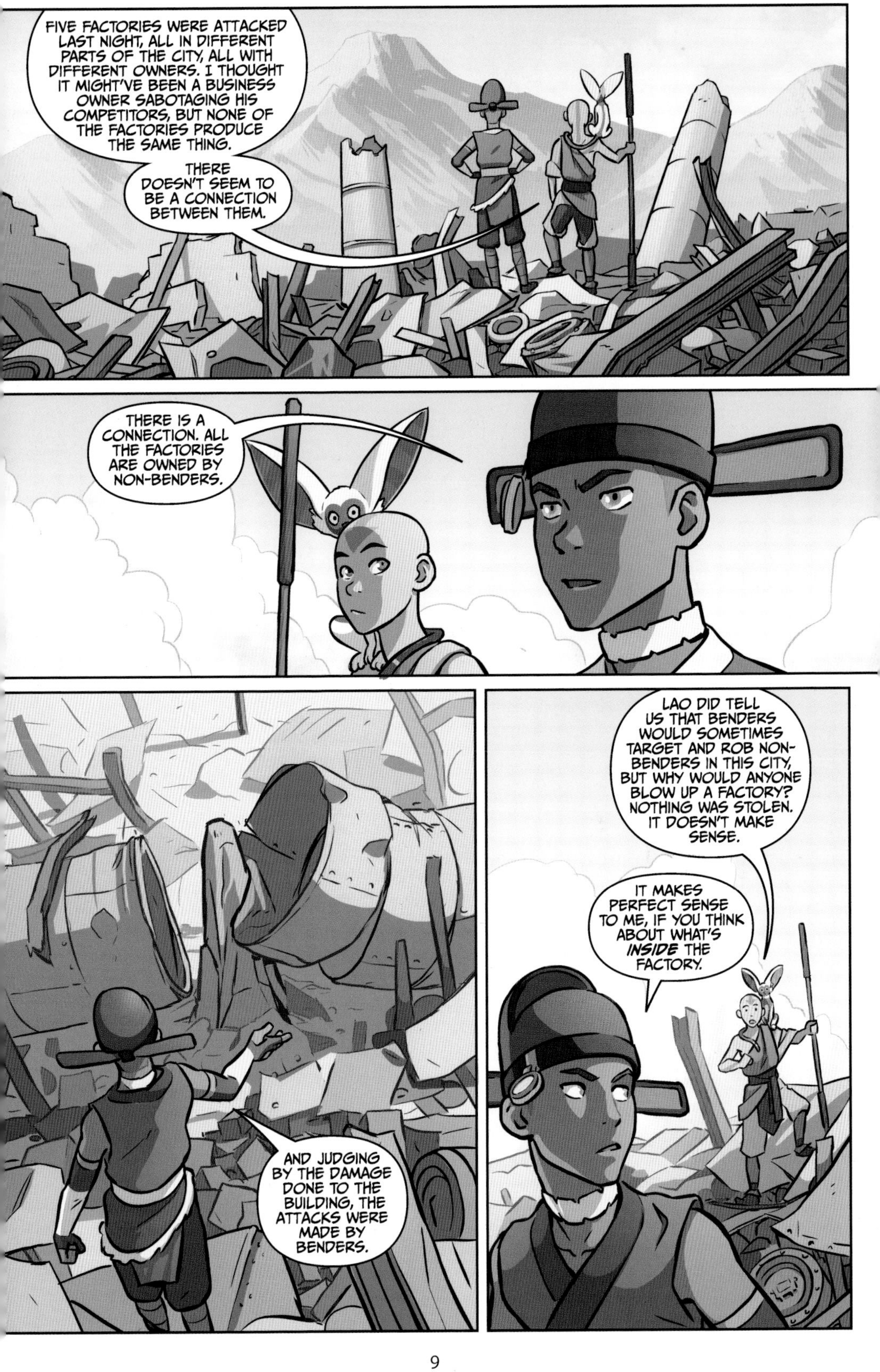

FIVE FACTORIES WERE ATTACKED LAST NIGHT, ALL IN DIFFERENT PARTS OF THE CITY, ALL WITH DIFFERENT OWNERS. I THOUGHT IT MIGHT'VE BEEN A BUSINESS OWNER SABOTAGING HIS COMPETITORS, BUT NONE OF THE FACTORIES PRODUCE THE SAME THING.
THERE DOESN'T SEEM TO BE A CONNECTION BETWEEN THEM.
THERE IS A CONNECTION. ALL THE FACTORIES ARE OWNED BY NON-BENDERS.
AND JUDGING BY THE DAMAGE DONE TO THE BUILDING, THE ATTACKS WERE MADE BY BENDERS.
LAO DID TELL US THAT BENDERS WOULD SOMETIMES TARGET AND ROB NON-BENDERS IN THIS CITY, BUT WHY WOULD ANYONE BLOW UP A FACTORY? NOTHING WAS STOLEN. IT DOESN'T MAKE SENSE.
IT MAKES PERFECT SENSE TO ME, IF YOU THINK ABOUT WHAT'S *INSIDE* THE FACTORY.

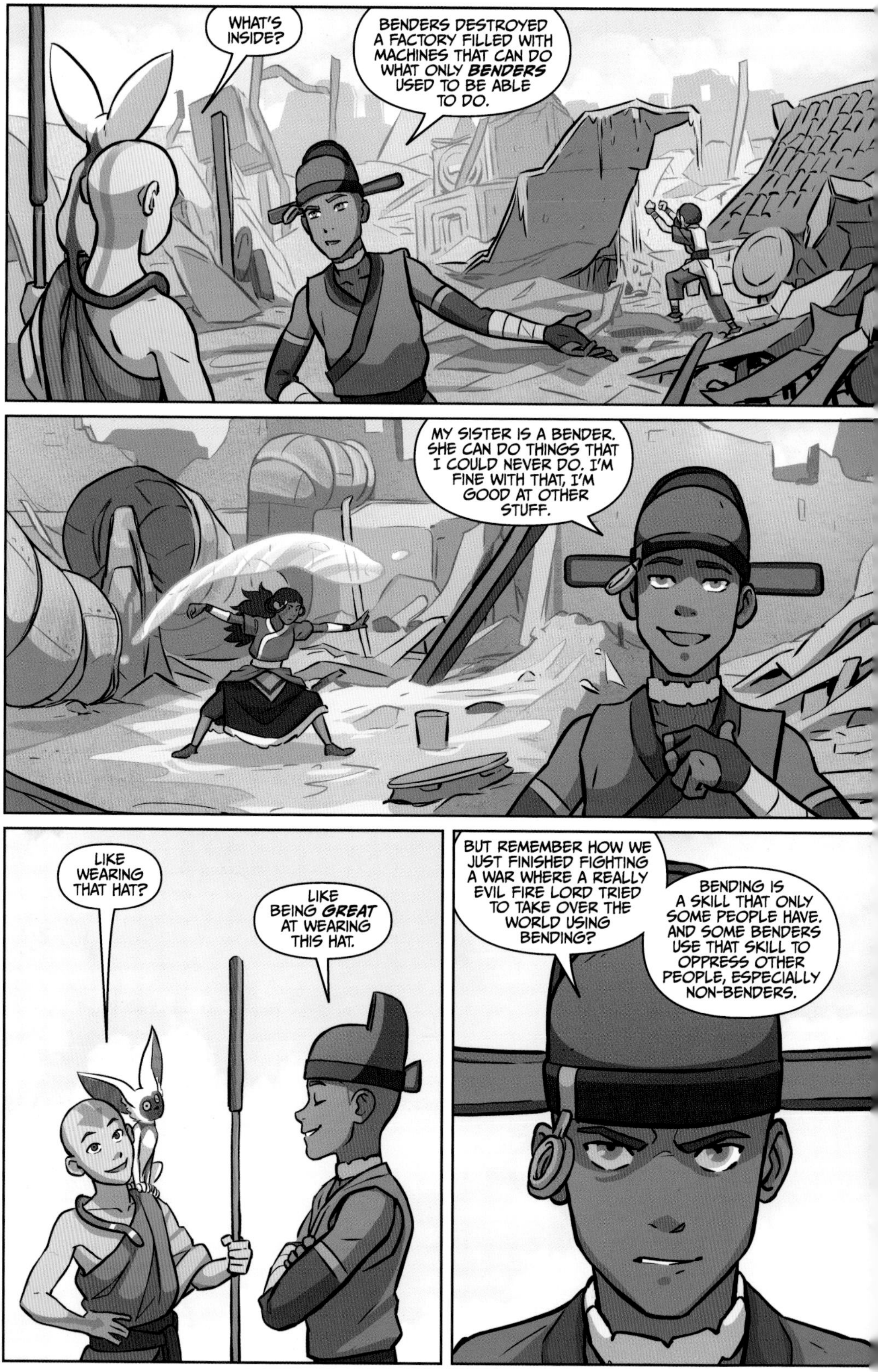
WHAT'S INSIDE?
BENDERS DESTROYED A FACTORY FILLED WITH MACHINES THAT CAN DO WHAT ONLY **BENDERS** USED TO BE ABLE TO DO.
MY SISTER IS A BENDER. SHE CAN DO THINGS THAT I COULD NEVER DO. I'M FINE WITH THAT, I'M GOOD AT OTHER STUFF.
LIKE WEARING THAT HAT?
LIKE BEING **GREAT** AT WEARING THIS HAT.
BUT REMEMBER HOW WE JUST FINISHED FIGHTING A WAR WHERE A REALLY EVIL FIRE LORD TRIED TO TAKE OVER THE WORLD USING BENDING?
BENDING IS A SKILL THAT ONLY SOME PEOPLE HAVE. AND SOME BENDERS USE THAT SKILL TO OPPRESS OTHER PEOPLE, ESPECIALLY NON-BENDERS.

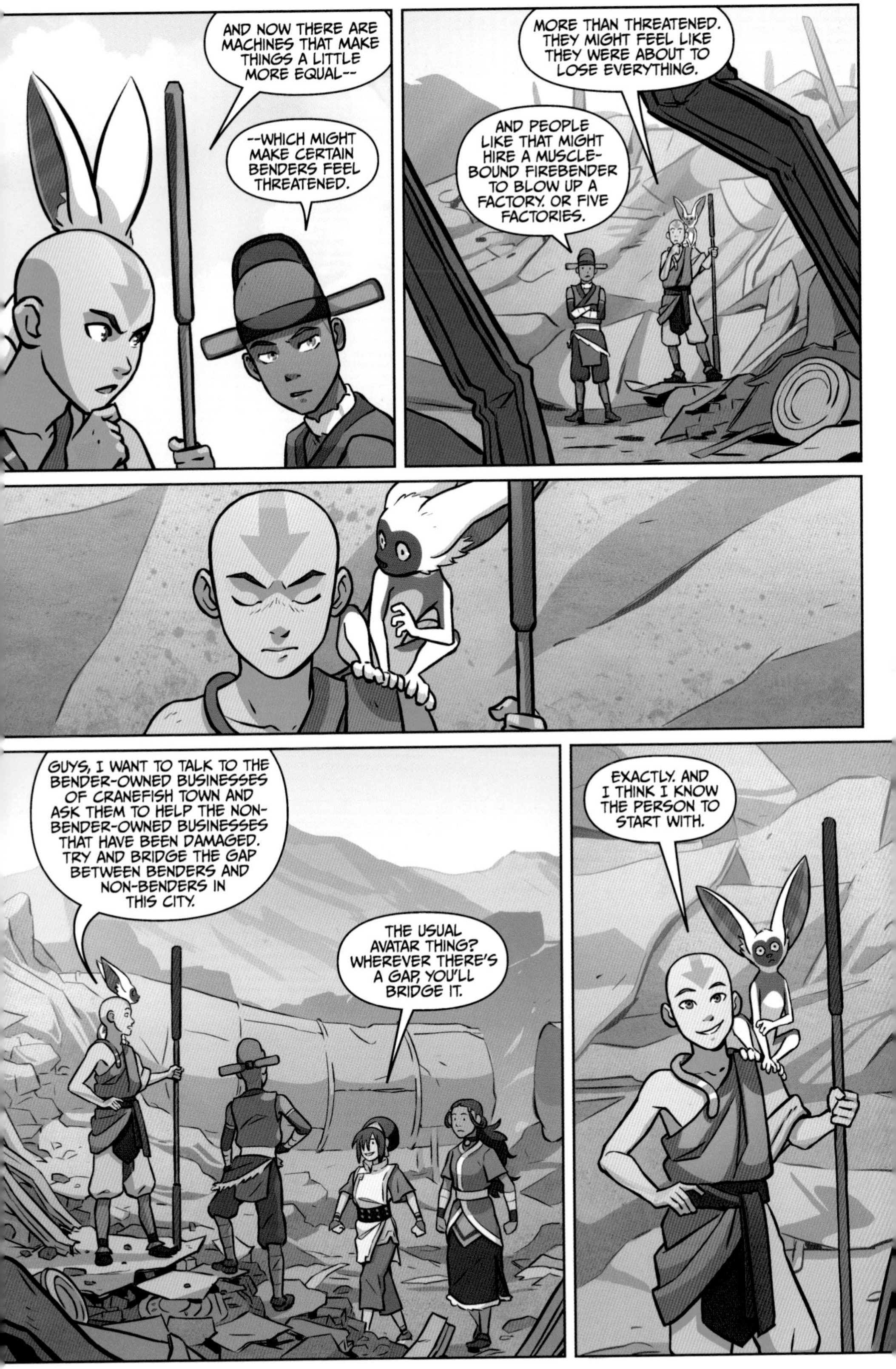
AND NOW THERE ARE MACHINES THAT MAKE THINGS A LITTLE MORE EQUAL--
--WHICH MIGHT MAKE CERTAIN BENDERS FEEL THREATENED.
MORE THAN THREATENED. THEY MIGHT FEEL LIKE THEY WERE ABOUT TO LOSE EVERYTHING.
AND PEOPLE LIKE THAT MIGHT HIRE A MUSCLE-BOUND FIREBENDER TO BLOW UP A FACTORY. OR FIVE FACTORIES.
GUYS, I WANT TO TALK TO THE BENDER-OWNED BUSINESSES OF CRANEFISH TOWN AND ASK THEM TO HELP THE NON-BENDER-OWNED BUSINESSES THAT HAVE BEEN DAMAGED. TRY AND BRIDGE THE GAP BETWEEN BENDERS AND NON-BENDERS IN THIS CITY.
THE USUAL AVATAR THING? WHEREVER THERE'S A GAP, YOU'LL BRIDGE IT.
EXACTLY. AND I THINK I KNOW THE PERSON TO START WITH.

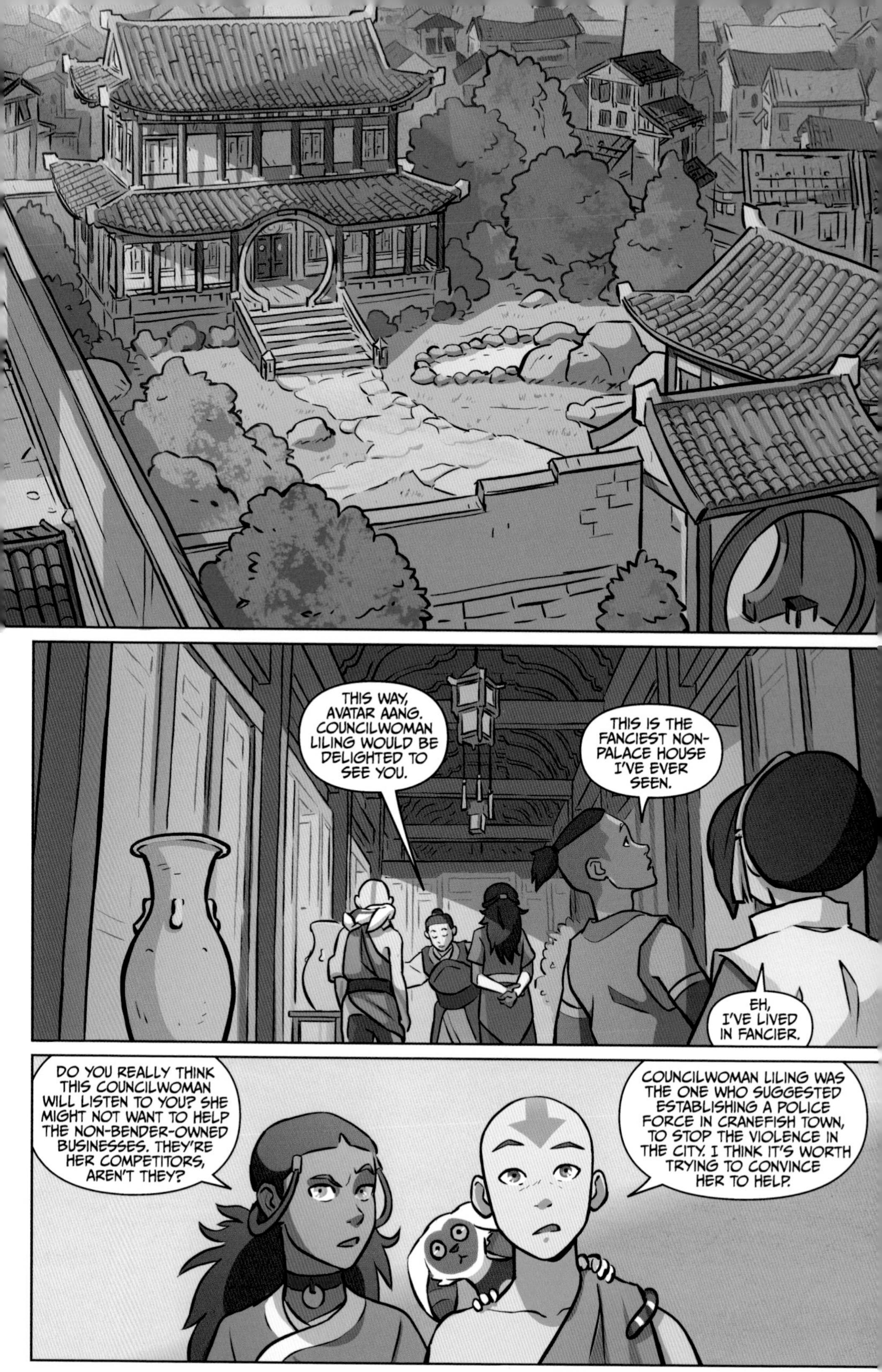
THIS WAY, AVATAR AANG. COUNCILWOMAN LILING WOULD BE DELIGHTED TO SEE YOU.
THIS IS THE FANCIEST NON-PALACE HOUSE I'VE EVER SEEN.
EH, I'VE LIVED IN FANCIER.
DO YOU REALLY THINK THIS COUNCILWOMAN WILL LISTEN TO YOU? SHE MIGHT NOT WANT TO HELP THE NON-BENDER-OWNED BUSINESSES. THEY'RE HER COMPETITORS, AREN'T THEY?
COUNCILWOMAN LILING WAS THE ONE WHO SUGGESTED ESTABLISHING A POLICE FORCE IN CRANEFISH TOWN, TO STOP THE VIOLENCE IN THE CITY. I THINK IT'S WORTH TRYING TO CONVINCE HER TO HELP.

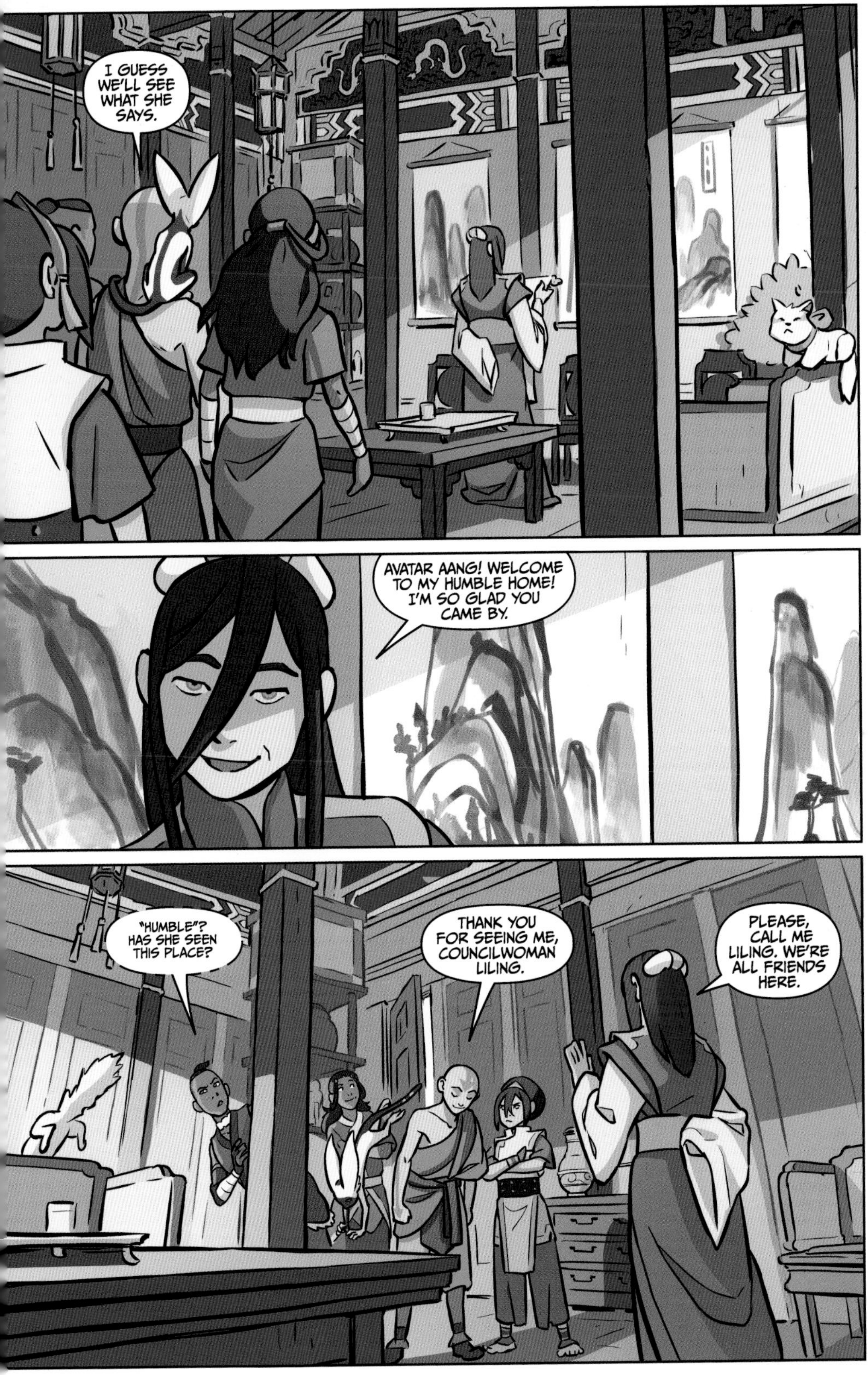
I GUESS WE'LL SEE WHAT SHE SAYS.
AVATAR AANG! WELCOME TO MY HUMBLE HOME! I'M SO GLAD YOU CAME BY.
"HUMBLE"? HAS SHE SEEN THIS PLACE?
THANK YOU FOR SEEING ME, COUNCILWOMAN LILING.
PLEASE, CALL ME LILING. WE'RE ALL FRIENDS HERE.

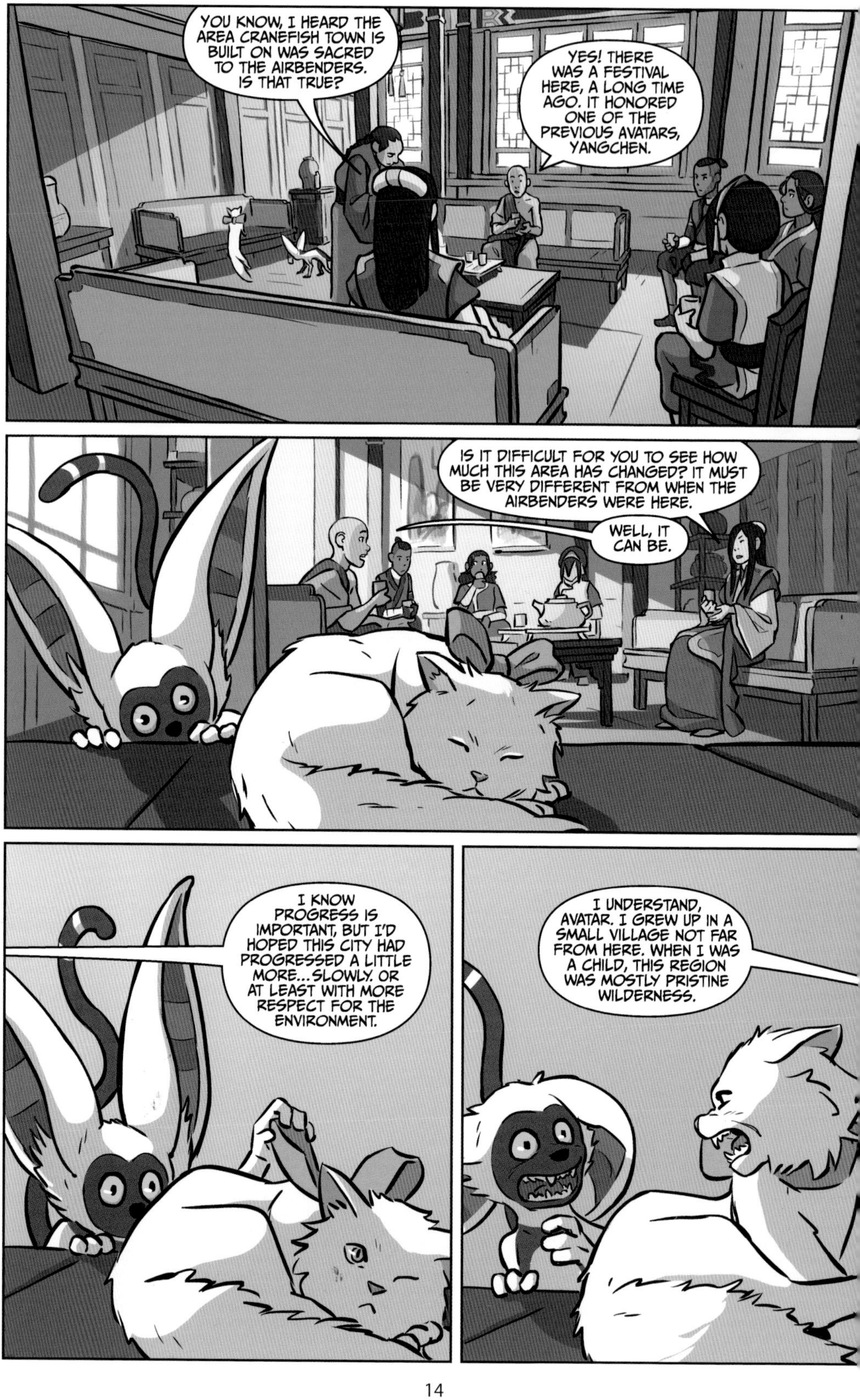
YOU KNOW, I HEARD THE AREA CRANEFISH TOWN IS BUILT ON WAS SACRED TO THE AIRBENDERS. IS THAT TRUE?
YES! THERE WAS A FESTIVAL HERE, A LONG TIME AGO. IT HONORED ONE OF THE PREVIOUS AVATARS, YANGCHEN.
IS IT DIFFICULT FOR YOU TO SEE HOW MUCH THIS AREA HAS CHANGED? IT MUST BE VERY DIFFERENT FROM WHEN THE AIRBENDERS WERE HERE.
WELL, IT CAN BE.
I KNOW PROGRESS IS IMPORTANT, BUT I'D HOPED THIS CITY HAD PROGRESSED A LITTLE MORE... SLOWLY. OR AT LEAST WITH MORE RESPECT FOR THE ENVIRONMENT.
I UNDERSTAND, AVATAR. I GREW UP IN A SMALL VILLAGE NOT FAR FROM HERE. WHEN I WAS A CHILD, THIS REGION WAS MOSTLY PRISTINE WILDERNESS.

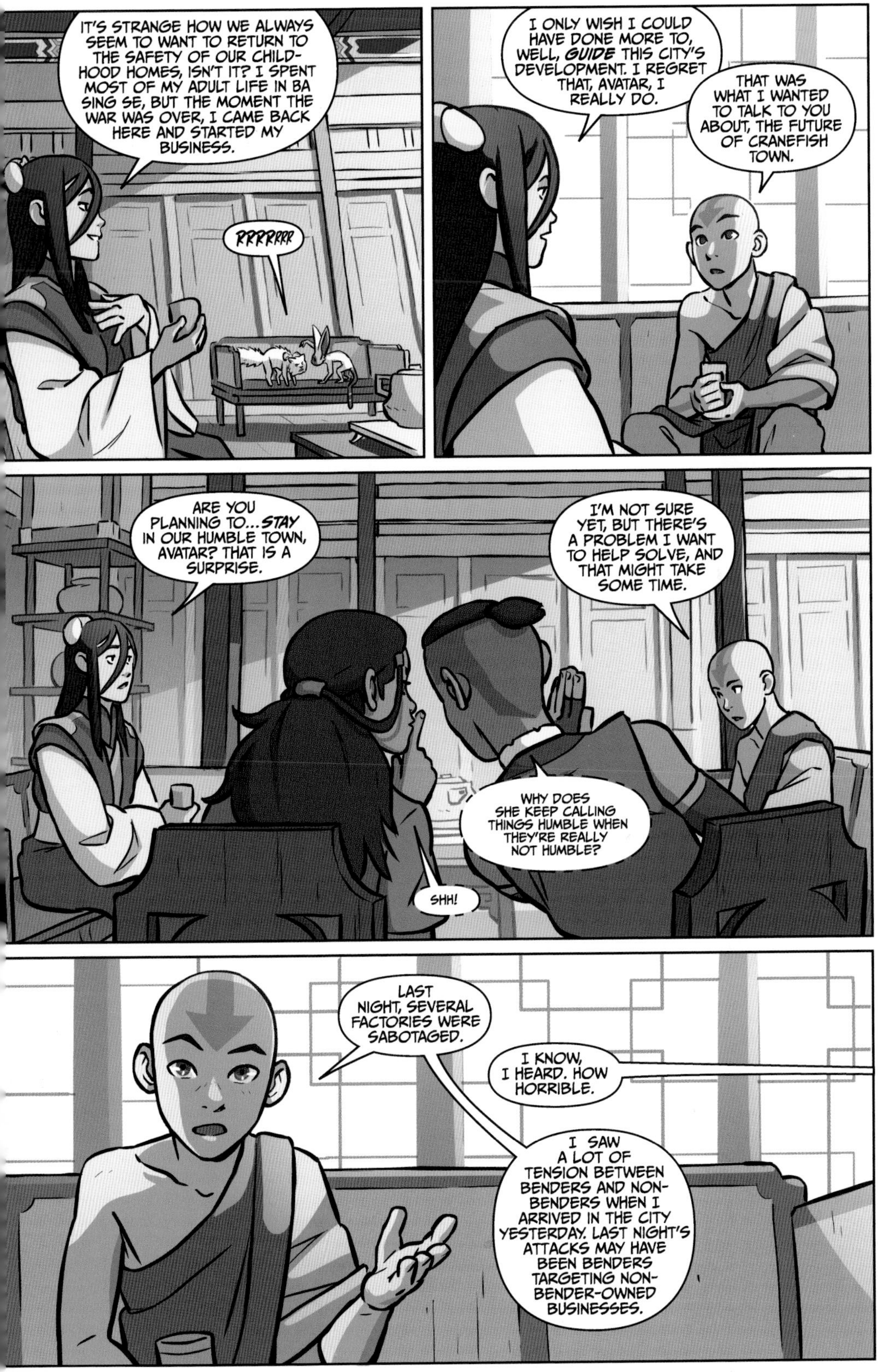

IT'S STRANGE HOW WE ALWAYS SEEM TO WANT TO RETURN TO THE SAFETY OF OUR CHILD-HOOD HOMES, ISN'T IT? I SPENT MOST OF MY ADULT LIFE IN BA SING SE, BUT THE MOMENT THE WAR WAS OVER, I CAME BACK HERE AND STARTED MY BUSINESS.
RRRRRRR
I ONLY WISH I COULD HAVE DONE MORE TO, WELL, ***GUIDE*** THIS CITY'S DEVELOPMENT. I REGRET THAT, AVATAR, I REALLY DO.
THAT WAS WHAT I WANTED TO TALK TO YOU ABOUT, THE FUTURE OF CRANEFISH TOWN.
ARE YOU PLANNING TO... ***STAY*** IN OUR HUMBLE TOWN, AVATAR? THAT IS A SURPRISE.
I'M NOT SURE YET, BUT THERE'S A PROBLEM I WANT TO HELP SOLVE, AND THAT MIGHT TAKE SOME TIME.
WHY DOES SHE KEEP CALLING THINGS HUMBLE WHEN THEY'RE REALLY NOT HUMBLE?
SHH!
LAST NIGHT, SEVERAL FACTORIES WERE SABOTAGED.
I KNOW, I HEARD. HOW HORRIBLE.
I SAW A LOT OF TENSION BETWEEN BENDERS AND NON-BENDERS WHEN I ARRIVED IN THE CITY YESTERDAY. LAST NIGHT'S ATTACKS MAY HAVE BEEN BENDERS TARGETING NON-BENDER-OWNED BUSINESSES.

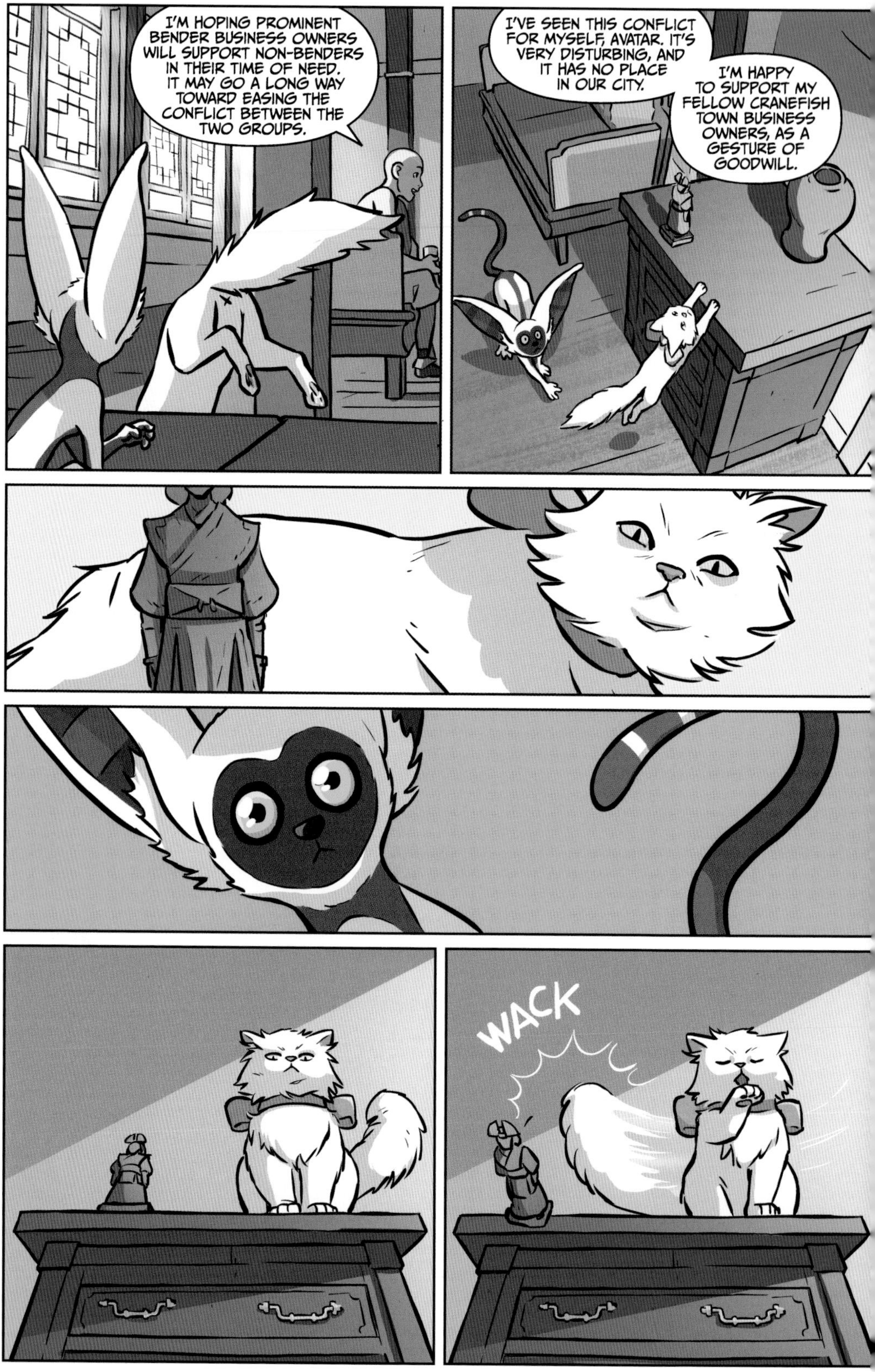
I'M HOPING PROMINENT BENDER BUSINESS OWNERS WILL SUPPORT NON-BENDERS IN THEIR TIME OF NEED. IT MAY GO A LONG WAY TOWARD EASING THE CONFLICT BETWEEN THE TWO GROUPS.
I'VE SEEN THIS CONFLICT FOR MYSELF, AVATAR. IT'S VERY DISTURBING, AND IT HAS NO PLACE IN OUR CITY.
I'M HAPPY TO SUPPORT MY FELLOW CRANEFISH TOWN BUSINESS OWNERS, AS A GESTURE OF GOODWILL.
WACK

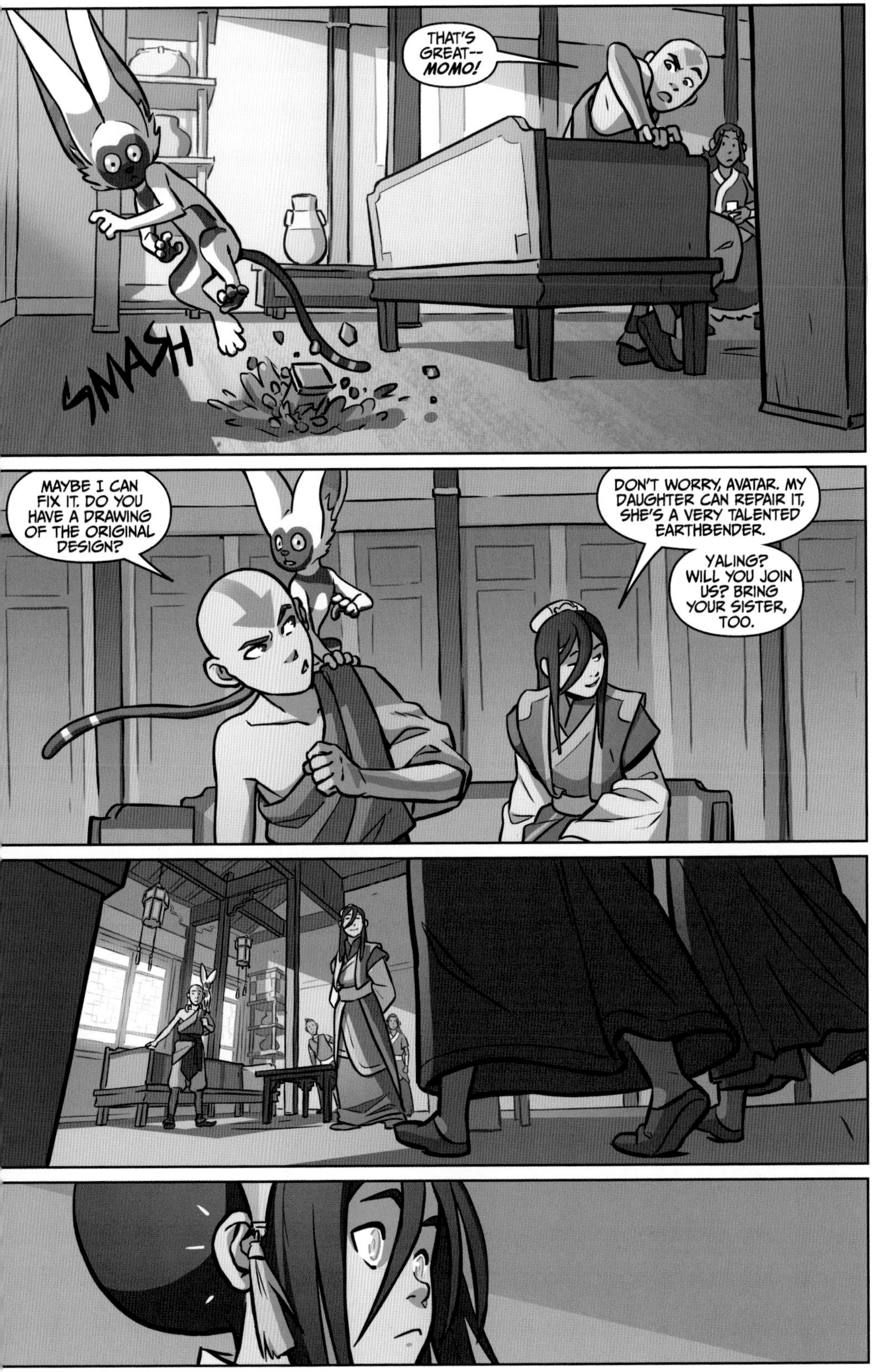
THAT'S GREAT-- MOMO!
SMASH
MAYBE I CAN FIX IT. DO YOU HAVE A DRAWING OF THE ORIGINAL DESIGN?
DON'T WORRY, AVATAR. MY DAUGHTER CAN REPAIR IT, SHE'S A VERY TALENTED EARTHBENDER.
YALING? WILL YOU JOIN US? BRING YOUR SISTER, TOO.

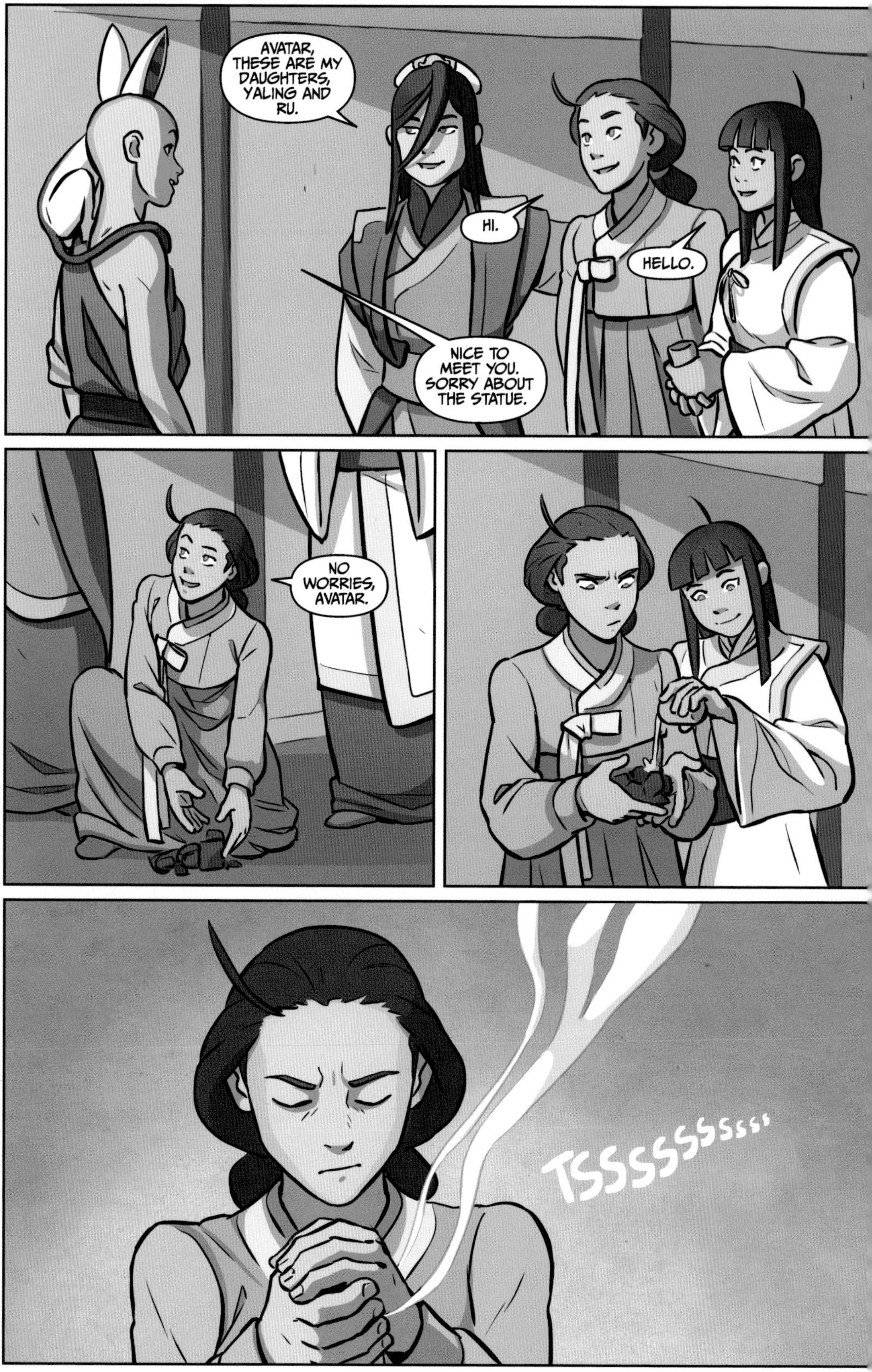
AVATAR, THESE ARE MY DAUGHTERS, YALING AND RU.
HI.
HELLO.
NICE TO MEET YOU. SORRY ABOUT THE STATUE.
NO WORRIES, AVATAR.
TSSSSSSsss

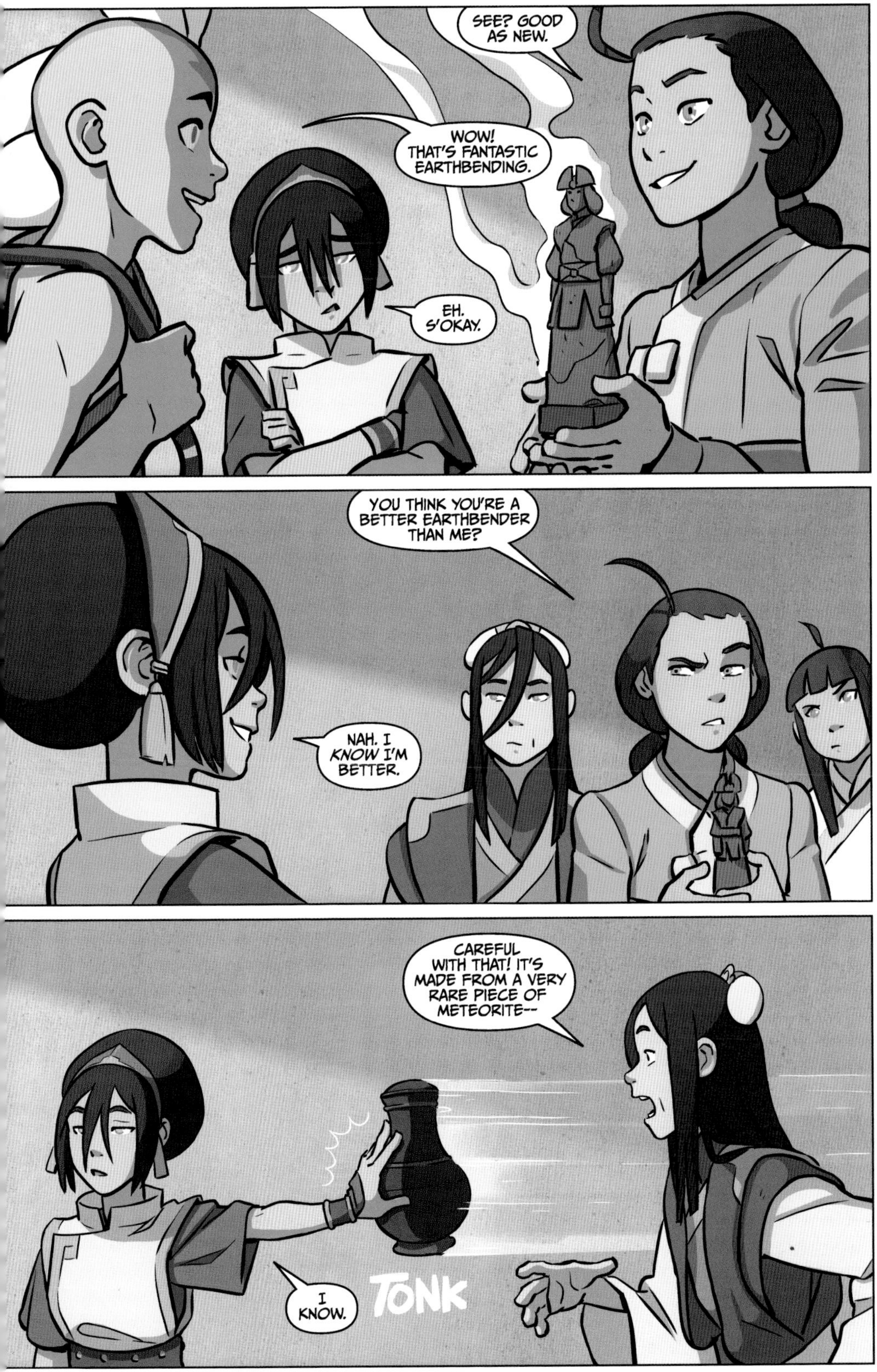
SEE? GOOD AS NEW.
WOW! THAT'S FANTASTIC EARTHBENDING.
EH. S'OKAY.
YOU THINK YOU'RE A BETTER EARTHBENDER THAN ME?
NAH. I KNOW I'M BETTER.
CAREFUL WITH THAT! IT'S MADE FROM A VERY RARE PIECE OF METEORITE--
I KNOW.
TONK

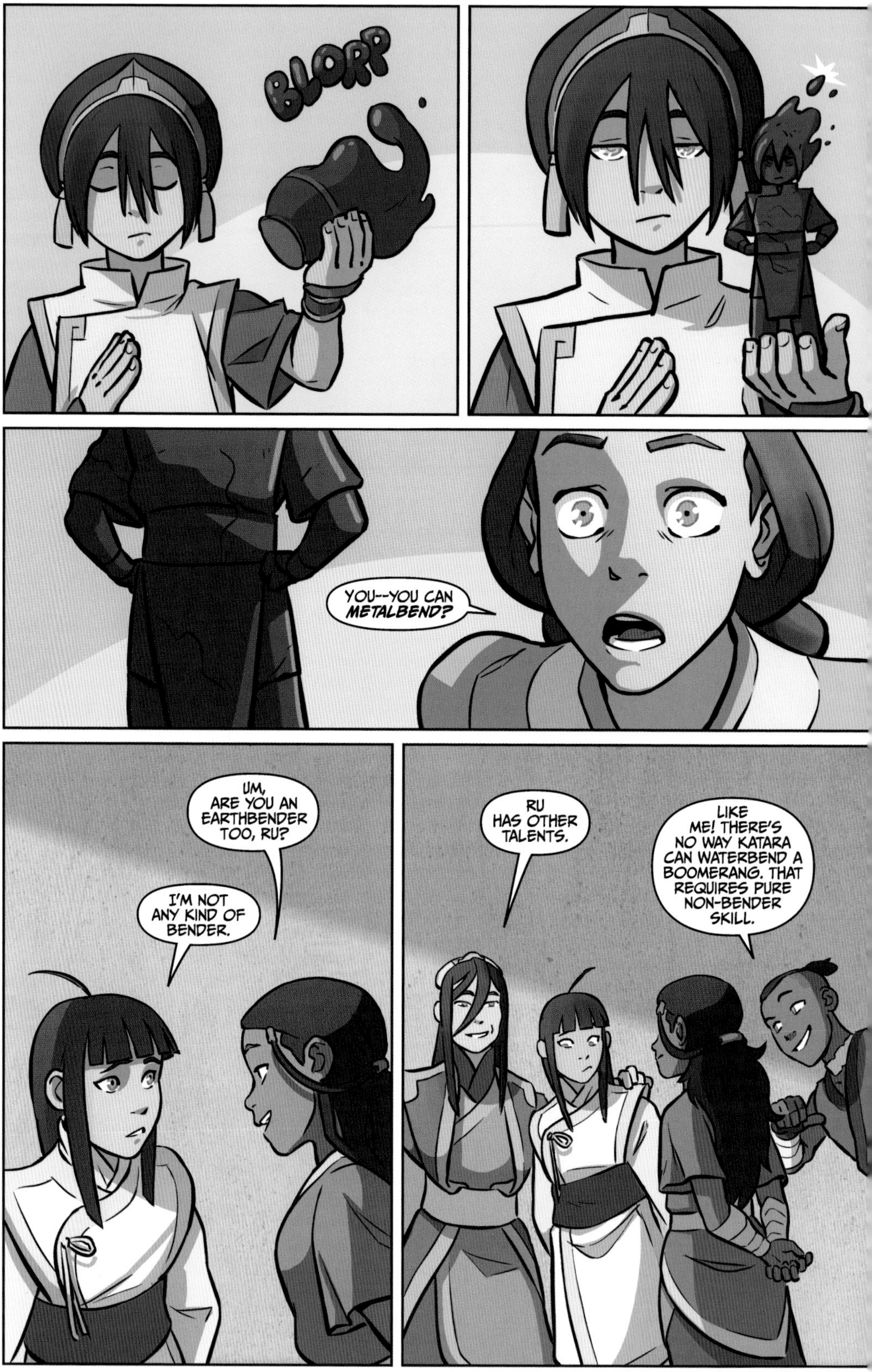
BLORP
YOU--YOU CAN *METALBEND?*
UM, ARE YOU AN EARTHBENDER TOO, RU?
I'M NOT ANY KIND OF BENDER.
RU HAS OTHER TALENTS.
LIKE ME! THERE'S NO WAY KATARA CAN WATERBEND A BOOMERANG. THAT REQUIRES PURE NON-BENDER SKILL.

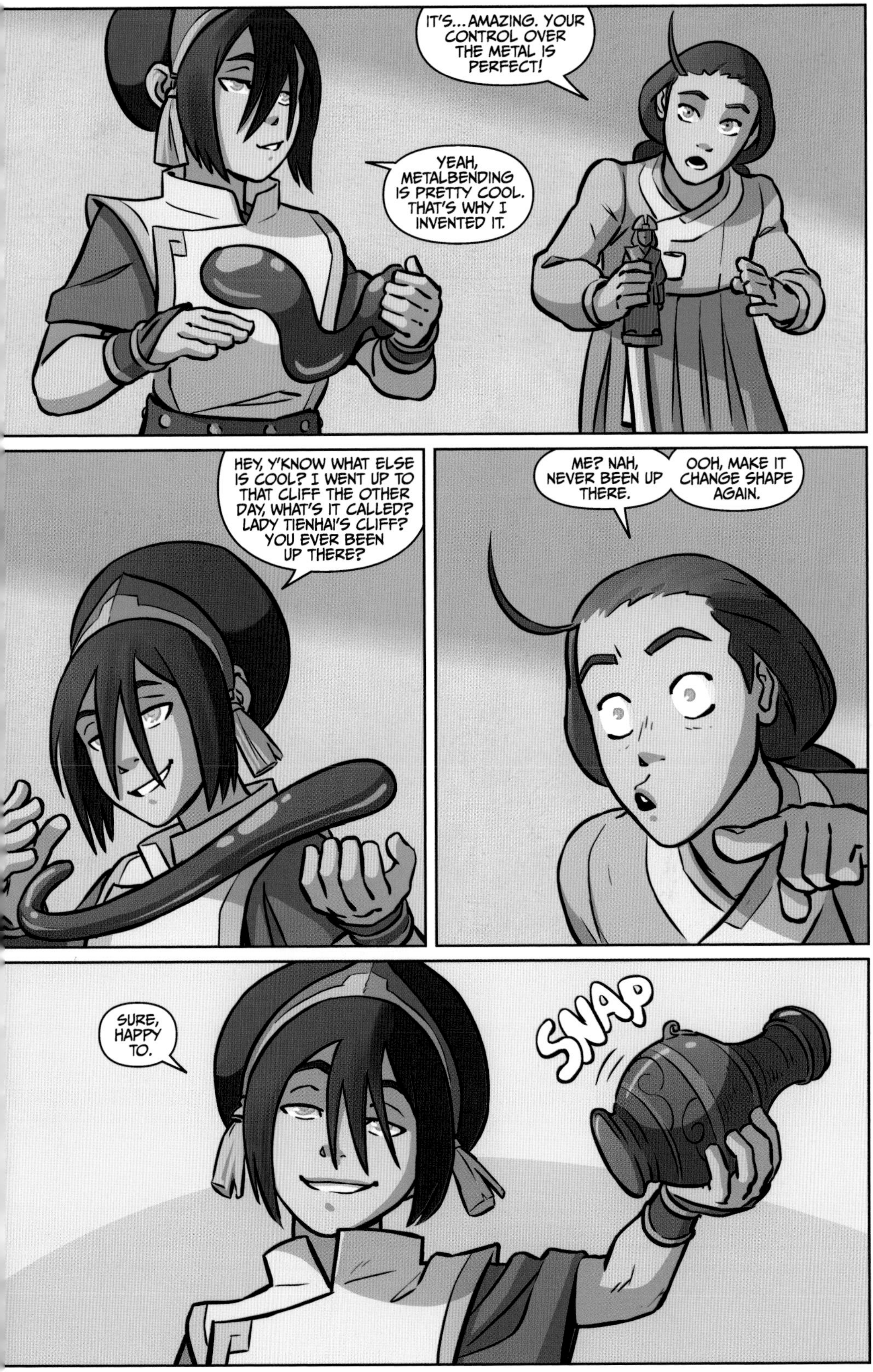
IT'S... AMAZING. YOUR CONTROL OVER THE METAL IS PERFECT!
YEAH, METALBENDING IS PRETTY COOL. THAT'S WHY I INVENTED IT.
HEY, Y'KNOW WHAT ELSE IS COOL? I WENT UP TO THAT CLIFF THE OTHER DAY, WHAT'S IT CALLED? LADY TIENHAI'S CLIFF? YOU EVER BEEN UP THERE?
ME? NAH, NEVER BEEN UP THERE.
OOH, MAKE IT CHANGE SHAPE AGAIN.
SURE, HAPPY TO.
SNAP

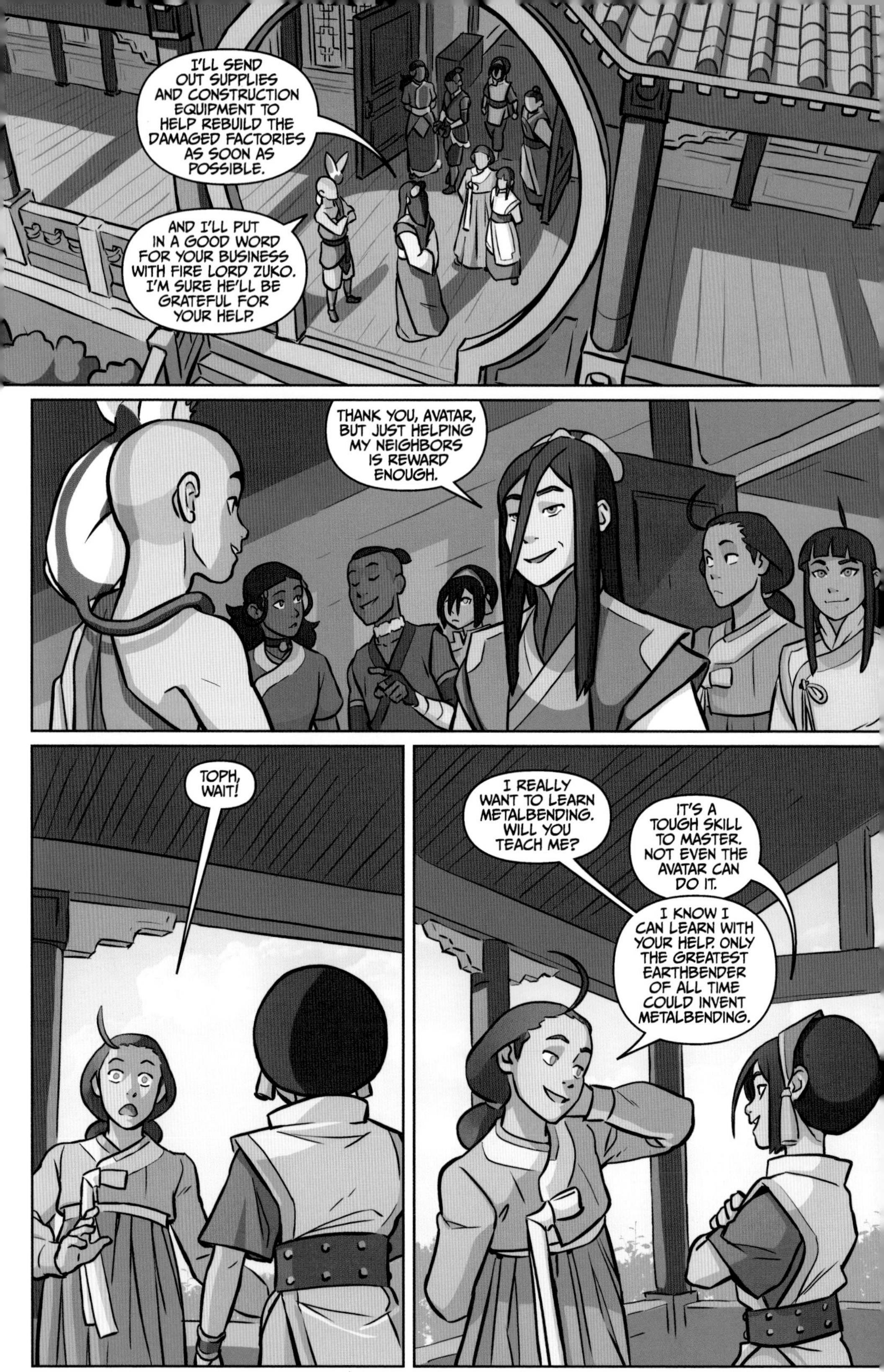
I'LL SEND OUT SUPPLIES AND CONSTRUCTION EQUIPMENT TO HELP REBUILD THE DAMAGED FACTORIES AS SOON AS POSSIBLE.
AND I'LL PUT IN A GOOD WORD FOR YOUR BUSINESS WITH FIRE LORD ZUKO. I'M SURE HE'LL BE GRATEFUL FOR YOUR HELP.
THANK YOU, AVATAR, BUT JUST HELPING MY NEIGHBORS IS REWARD ENOUGH.
TOPH, WAIT!
I REALLY WANT TO LEARN METALBENDING. WILL YOU TEACH ME?
IT'S A TOUGH SKILL TO MASTER. NOT EVEN THE AVATAR CAN DO IT.
I KNOW I CAN LEARN WITH YOUR HELP. ONLY THE GREATEST EARTHBENDER OF ALL TIME COULD INVENT METALBENDING.

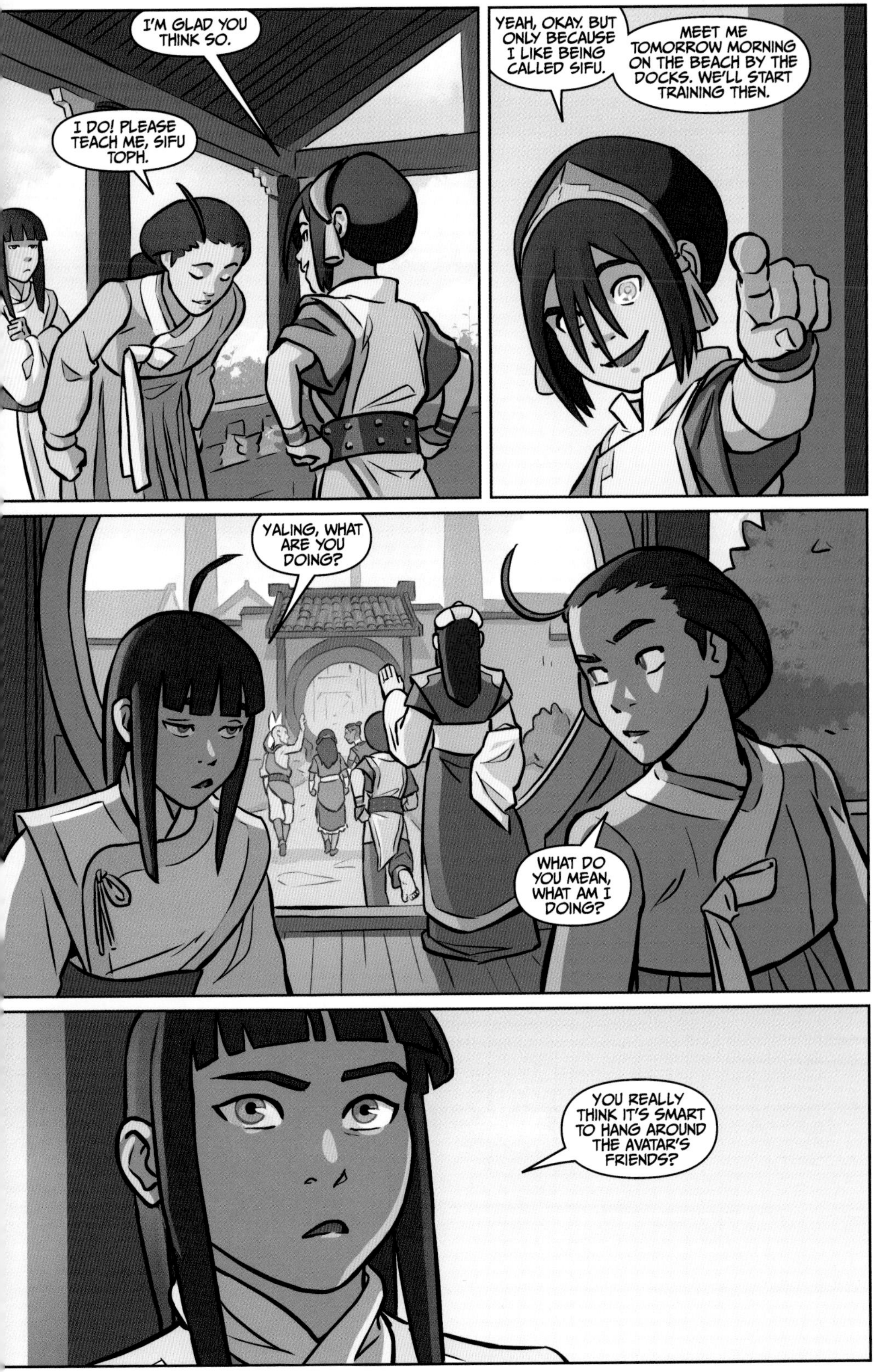
I'M GLAD YOU THINK SO.
I DO! PLEASE TEACH ME, SIFU TOPH.
YEAH, OKAY. BUT ONLY BECAUSE I LIKE BEING CALLED SIFU.
MEET ME TOMORROW MORNING ON THE BEACH BY THE DOCKS. WE'LL START TRAINING THEN.
YALING, WHAT ARE YOU DOING?
WHAT DO YOU MEAN, WHAT AM I DOING?
YOU REALLY THINK IT'S SMART TO HANG AROUND THE AVATAR'S FRIENDS?

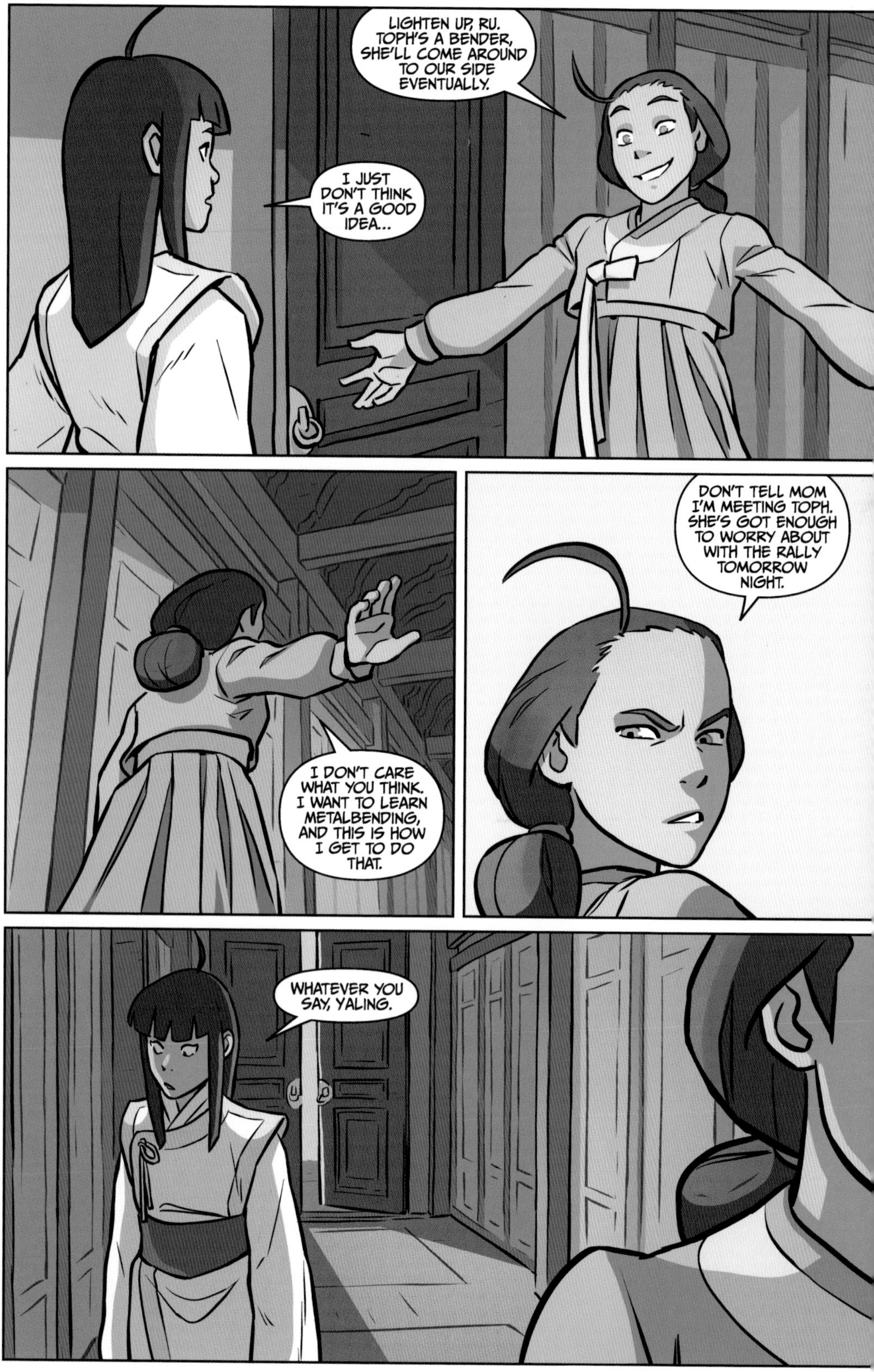
LIGHTEN UP, RU. TOPH'S A BENDER, SHE'LL COME AROUND TO OUR SIDE EVENTUALLY.
I JUST DON'T THINK IT'S A GOOD IDEA...
I DON'T CARE WHAT YOU THINK. I WANT TO LEARN METALBENDING, AND THIS IS HOW I GET TO DO THAT.
DON'T TELL MOM I'M MEETING TOPH. SHE'S GOT ENOUGH TO WORRY ABOUT WITH THE RALLY TOMORROW NIGHT.
WHATEVER YOU SAY, YALING.

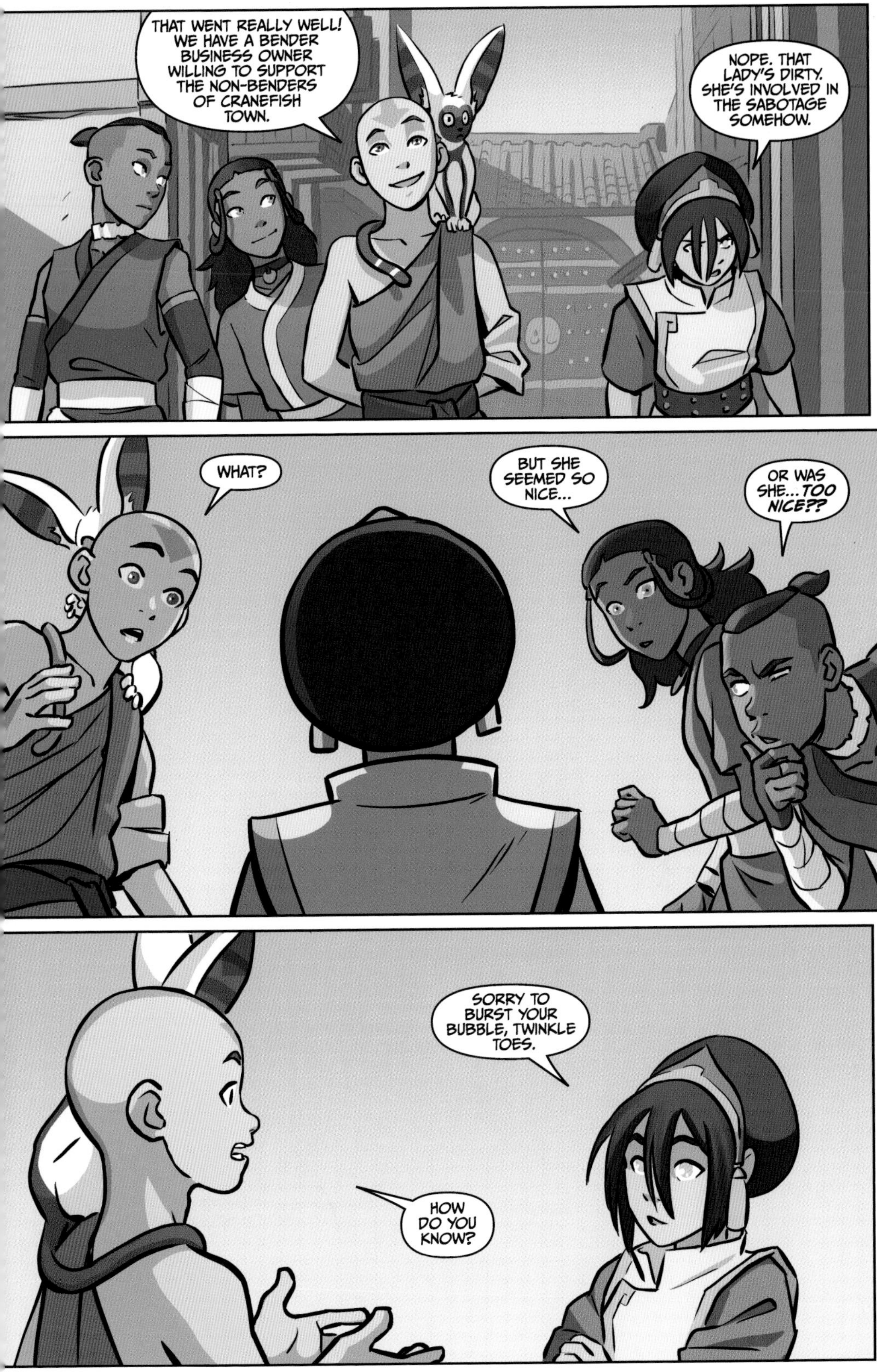
THAT WENT REALLY WELL! WE HAVE A BENDER BUSINESS OWNER WILLING TO SUPPORT THE NON-BENDERS OF CRANEFISH TOWN.
NOPE. THAT LADY'S DIRTY. SHE'S INVOLVED IN THE SABOTAGE SOMEHOW.
WHAT?
BUT SHE SEEMED SO NICE...
OR WAS SHE...*TOO NICE??*
SORRY TO BURST YOUR BUBBLE, TWINKLE TOES.
HOW DO YOU KNOW?

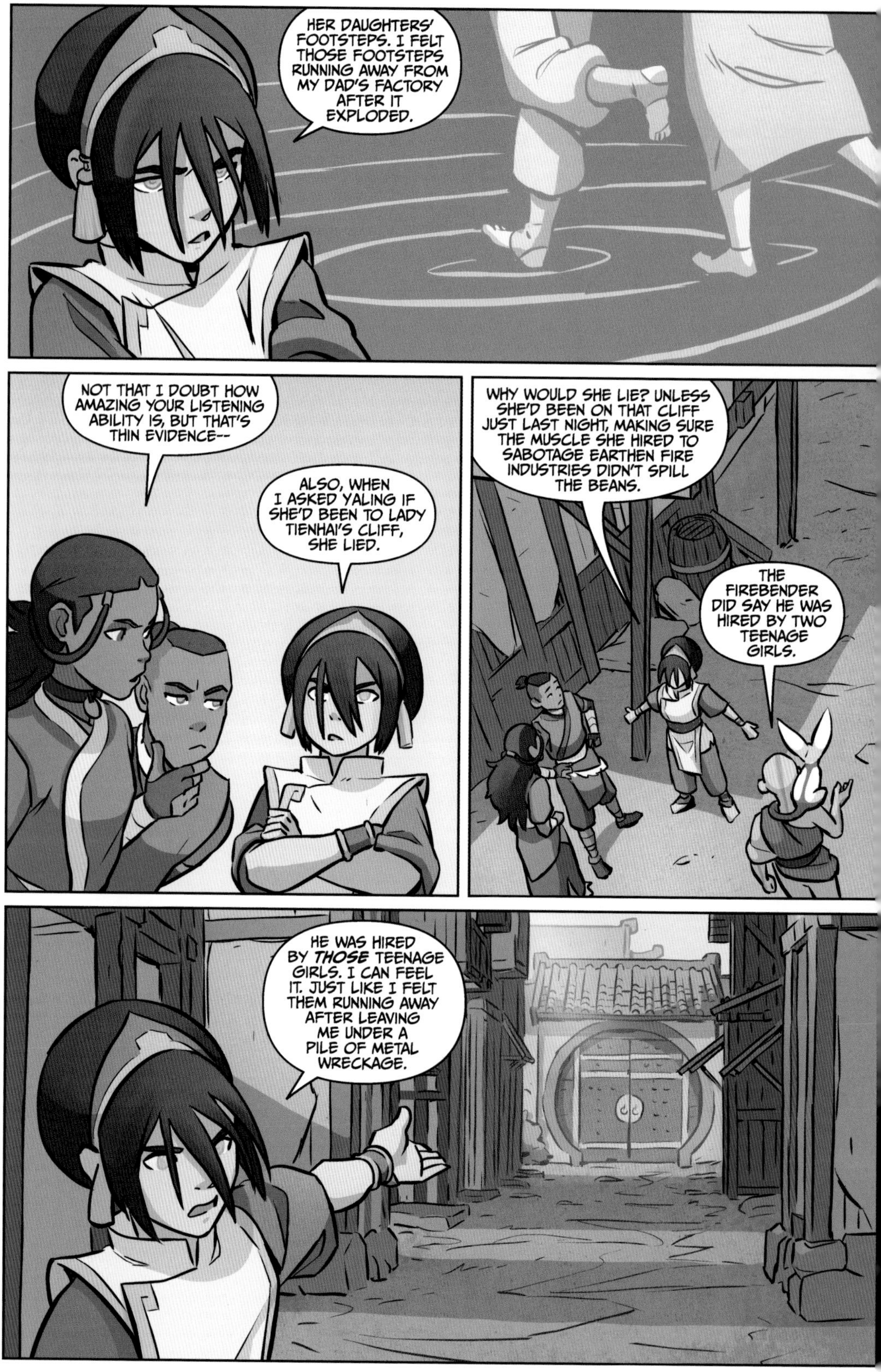
HER DAUGHTERS' FOOTSTEPS. I FELT THOSE FOOTSTEPS RUNNING AWAY FROM MY DAD'S FACTORY AFTER IT EXPLODED.
NOT THAT I DOUBT HOW AMAZING YOUR LISTENING ABILITY IS, BUT THAT'S THIN EVIDENCE--
ALSO, WHEN I ASKED YALING IF SHE'D BEEN TO LADY TIENHAI'S CLIFF, SHE LIED.
WHY WOULD SHE LIE? UNLESS SHE'D BEEN ON THAT CLIFF JUST LAST NIGHT, MAKING SURE THE MUSCLE SHE HIRED TO SABOTAGE EARTHEN FIRE INDUSTRIES DIDN'T SPILL THE BEANS.
THE FIREBENDER DID SAY HE WAS HIRED BY TWO TEENAGE GIRLS.
HE WAS HIRED BY *THOSE* TEENAGE GIRLS. I CAN FEEL IT. JUST LIKE I FELT THEM RUNNING AWAY AFTER LEAVING ME UNDER A PILE OF METAL WRECKAGE.

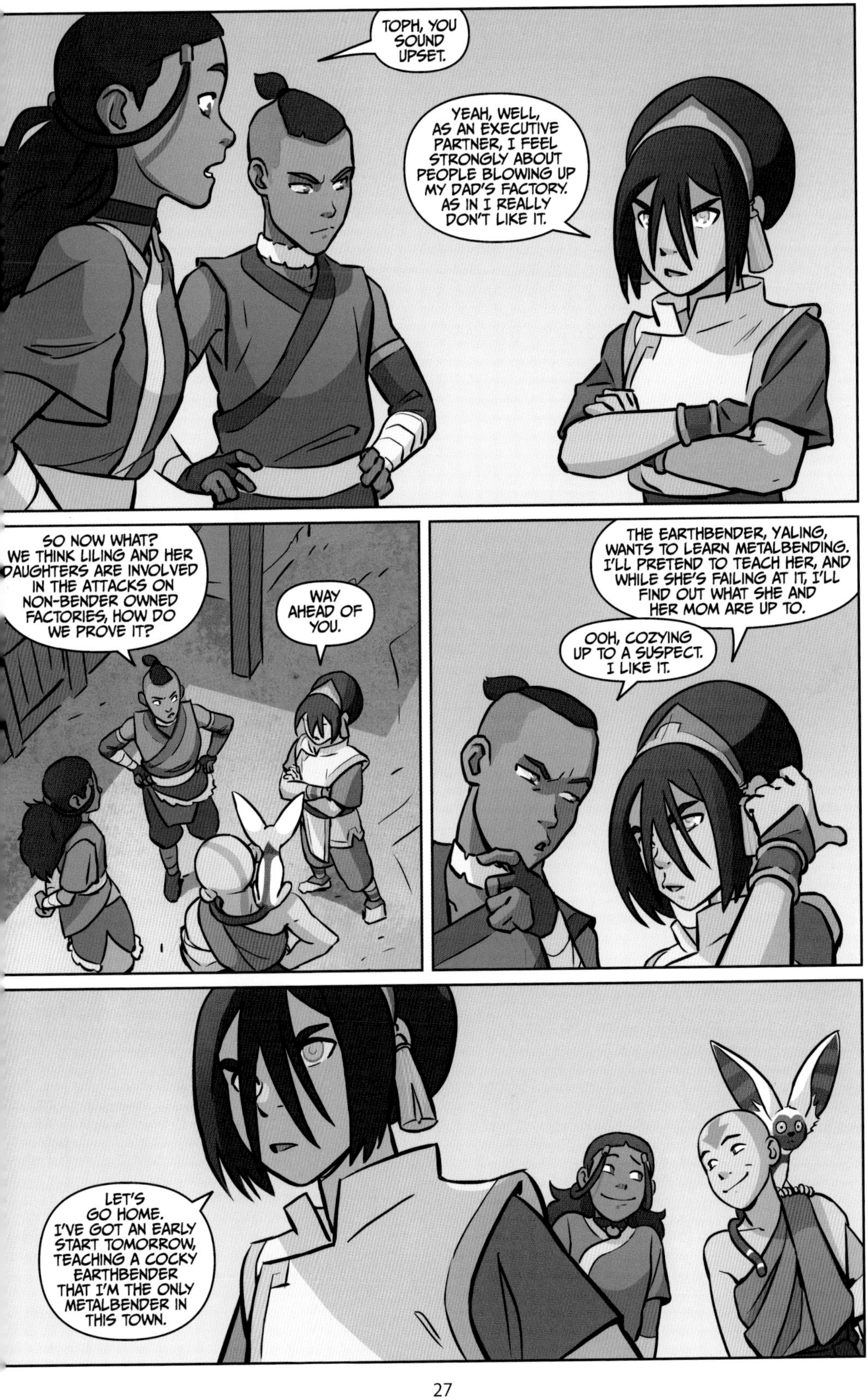
TOPH, YOU SOUND UPSET.
YEAH, WELL, AS AN EXECUTIVE PARTNER, I FEEL STRONGLY ABOUT PEOPLE BLOWING UP MY DAD'S FACTORY. AS IN I REALLY DON'T LIKE IT.
SO NOW WHAT? WE THINK LILING AND HER DAUGHTERS ARE INVOLVED IN THE ATTACKS ON NON-BENDER OWNED FACTORIES, HOW DO WE PROVE IT?
WAY AHEAD OF YOU.
THE EARTHBENDER, YALING, WANTS TO LEARN METALBENDING. I'LL PRETEND TO TEACH HER, AND WHILE SHE'S FAILING AT IT, I'LL FIND OUT WHAT SHE AND HER MOM ARE UP TO.
OOH, COZYING UP TO A SUSPECT. I LIKE IT.
LET'S GO HOME. I'VE GOT AN EARLY START TOMORROW, TEACHING A COCKY EARTHBENDER THAT I'M THE ONLY METALBENDER IN THIS TOWN.

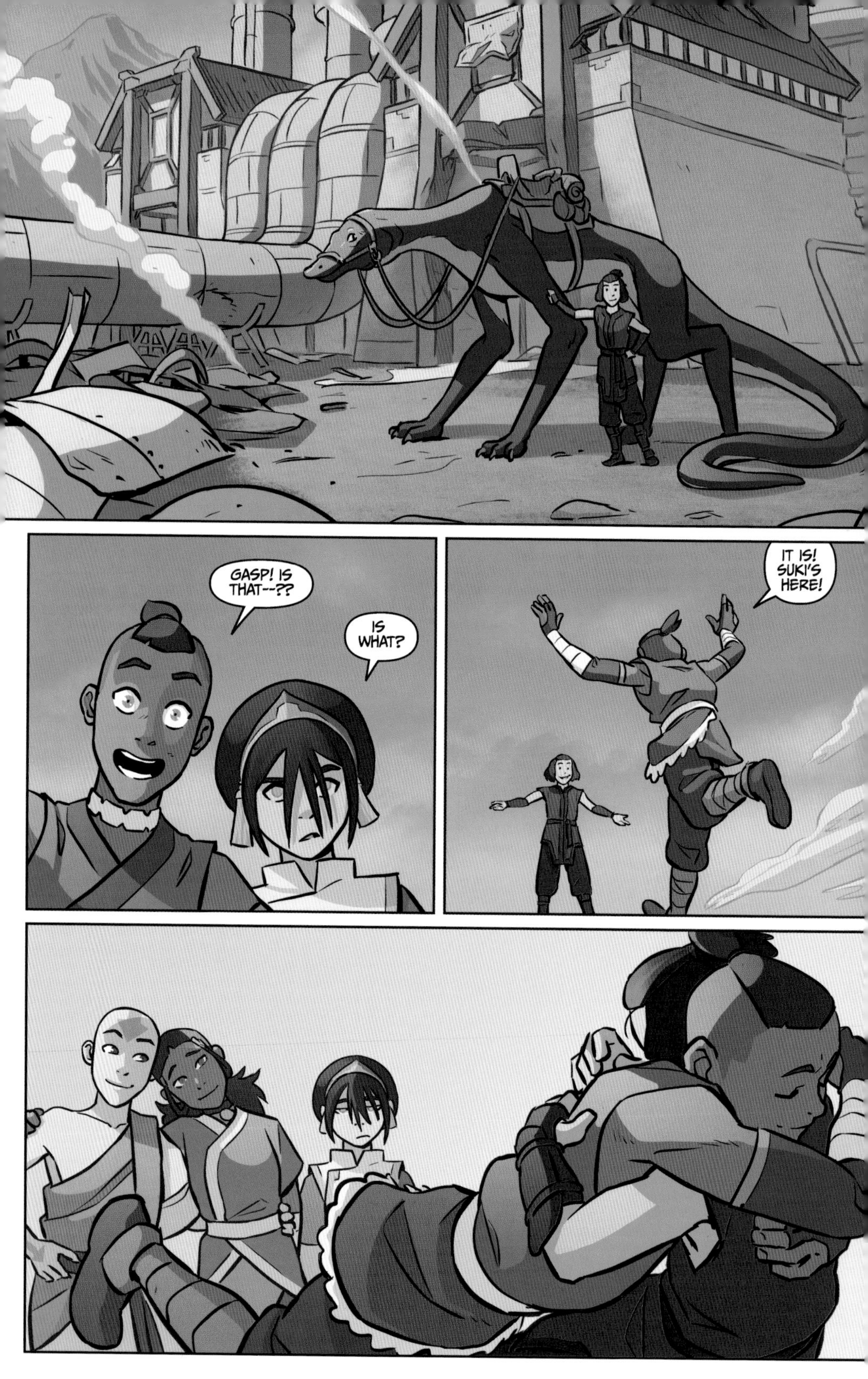
GASP! IS THAT--??
IS WHAT?
IT IS! SUKI'S HERE!

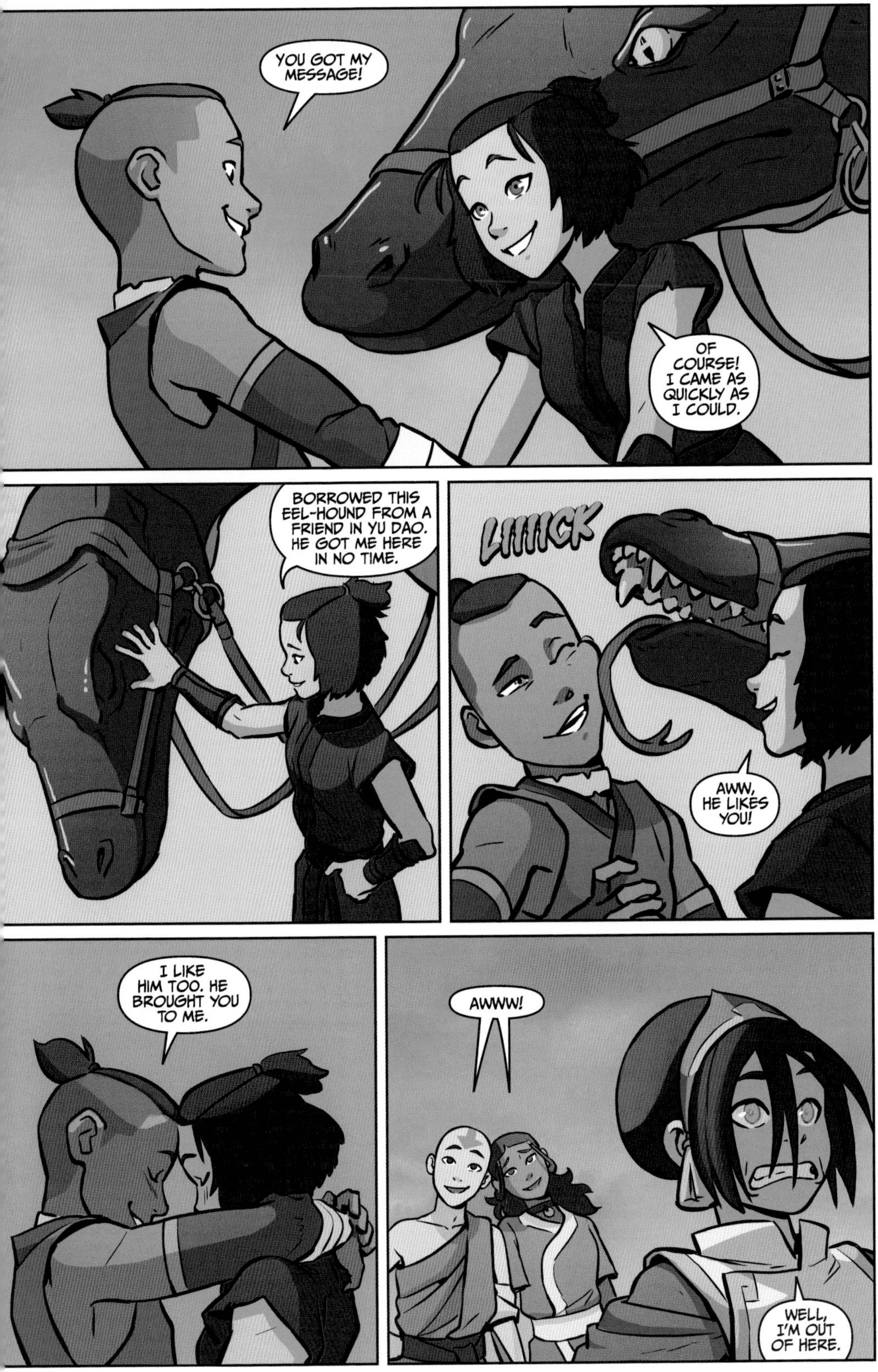
YOU GOT MY MESSAGE!
OF COURSE! I CAME AS QUICKLY AS I COULD.
BORROWED THIS EEL-HOUND FROM A FRIEND IN YU DAO. HE GOT ME HERE IN NO TIME.
LIIIICK
AWW, HE LIKES YOU!
I LIKE HIM TOO. HE BROUGHT YOU TO ME.
AWWW!
WELL, I'M OUT OF HERE.

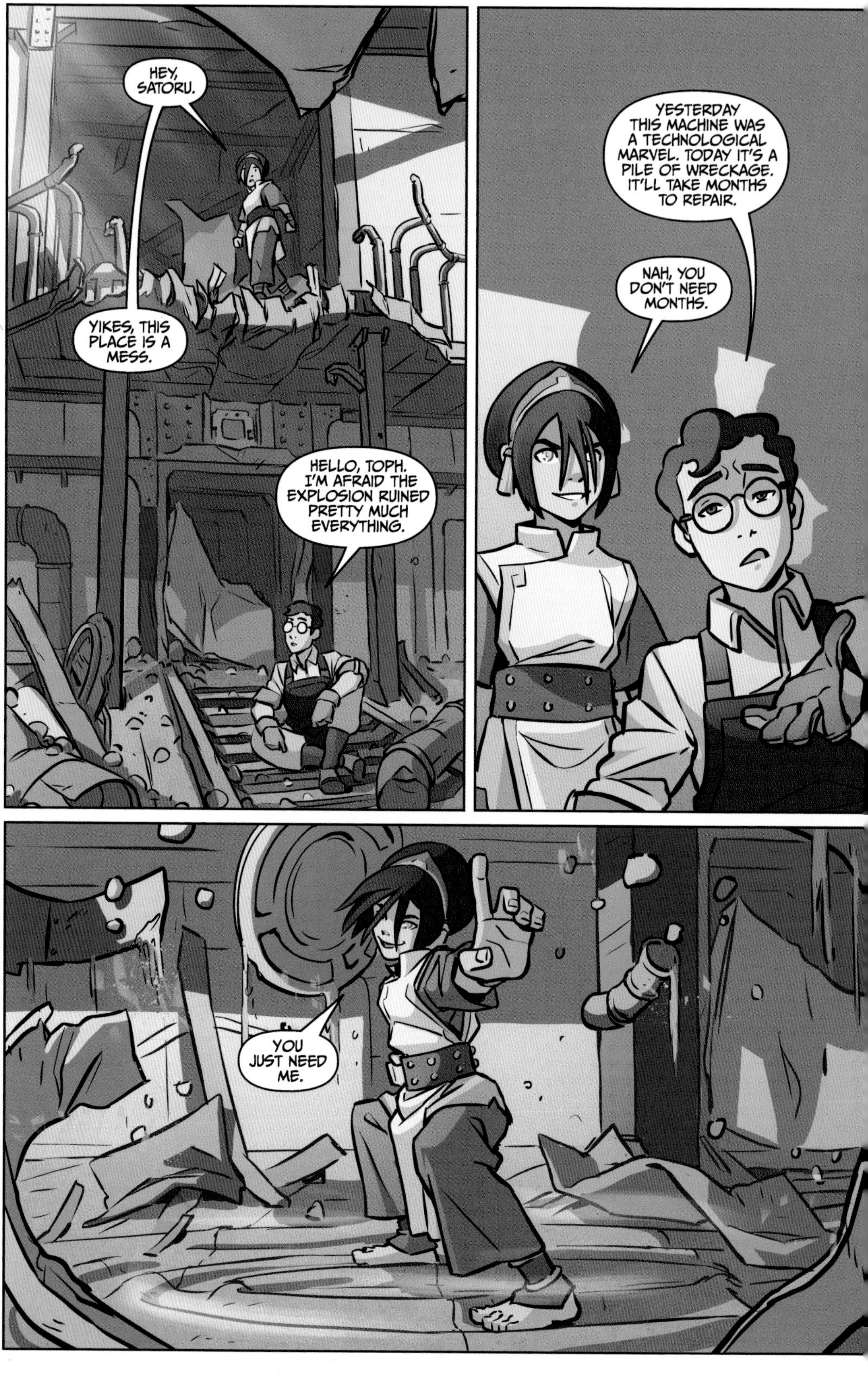
HEY, SATORU.
YIKES, THIS PLACE IS A MESS.
HELLO, TOPH. I'M AFRAID THE EXPLOSION RUINED PRETTY MUCH EVERYTHING.
YESTERDAY THIS MACHINE WAS A TECHNOLOGICAL MARVEL. TODAY IT'S A PILE OF WRECKAGE. IT'LL TAKE MONTHS TO REPAIR.
NAH, YOU DON'T NEED MONTHS.
YOU JUST NEED ME.

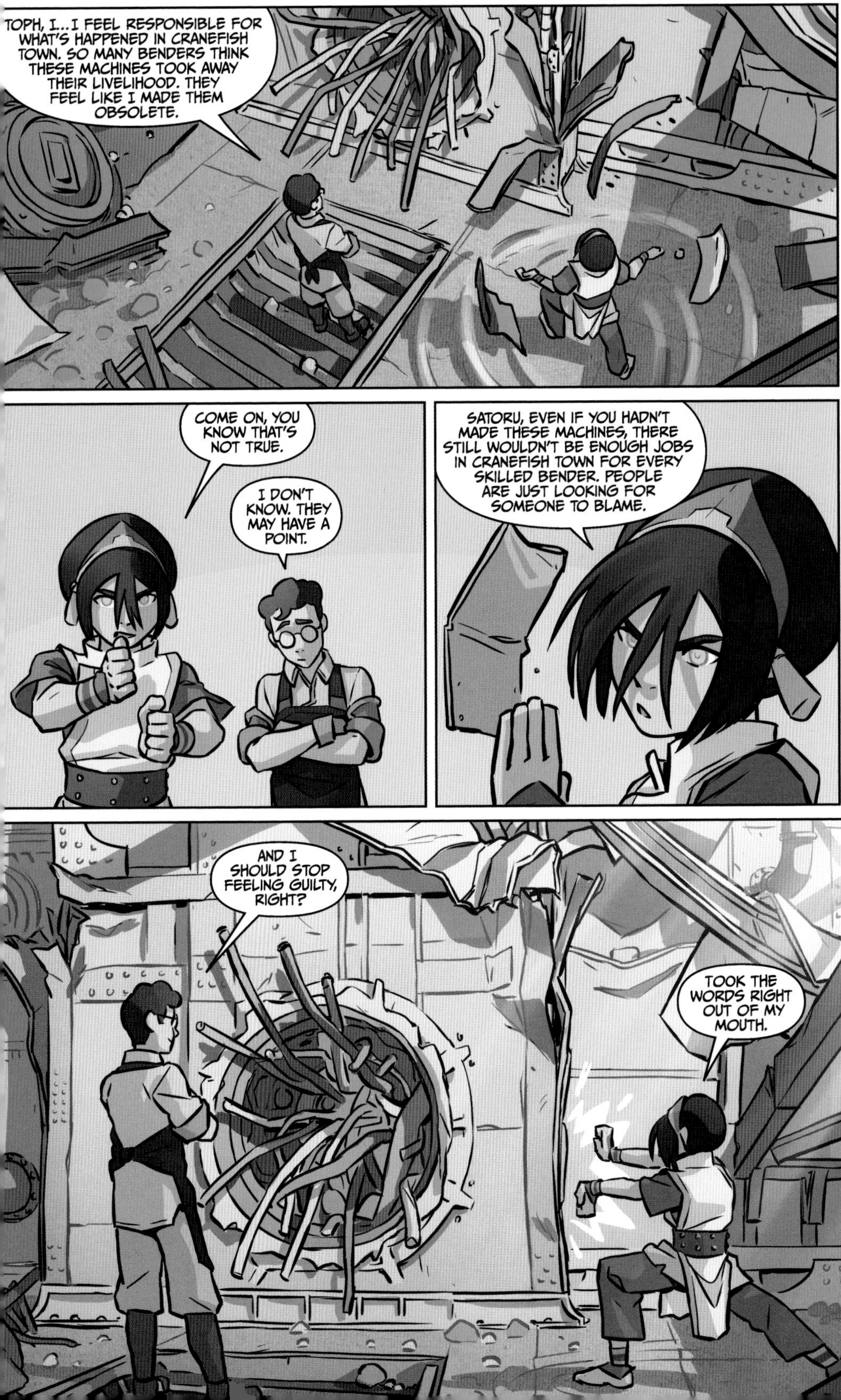
TOPH, I...I FEEL RESPONSIBLE FOR WHAT'S HAPPENED IN CRANEFISH TOWN. SO MANY BENDERS THINK THESE MACHINES TOOK AWAY THEIR LIVELIHOOD. THEY FEEL LIKE I MADE THEM OBSOLETE.
COME ON, YOU KNOW THAT'S NOT TRUE.
I DON'T KNOW. THEY MAY HAVE A POINT.
SATORU, EVEN IF YOU HADN'T MADE THESE MACHINES, THERE STILL WOULDN'T BE ENOUGH JOBS IN CRANEFISH TOWN FOR EVERY SKILLED BENDER. PEOPLE ARE JUST LOOKING FOR SOMEONE TO BLAME.
AND I SHOULD STOP FEELING GUILTY, RIGHT?
TOOK THE WORDS RIGHT OUT OF MY MOUTH.

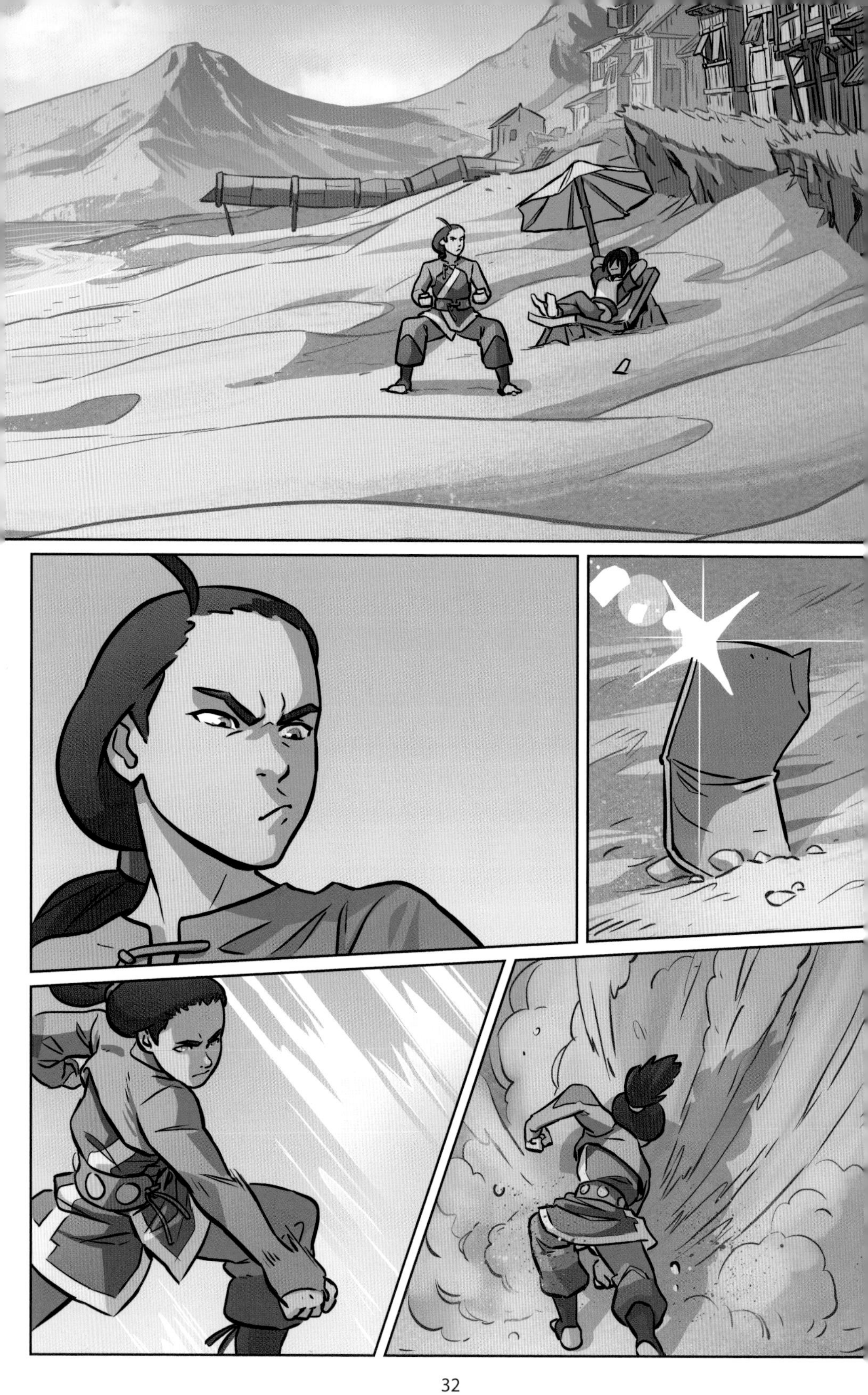

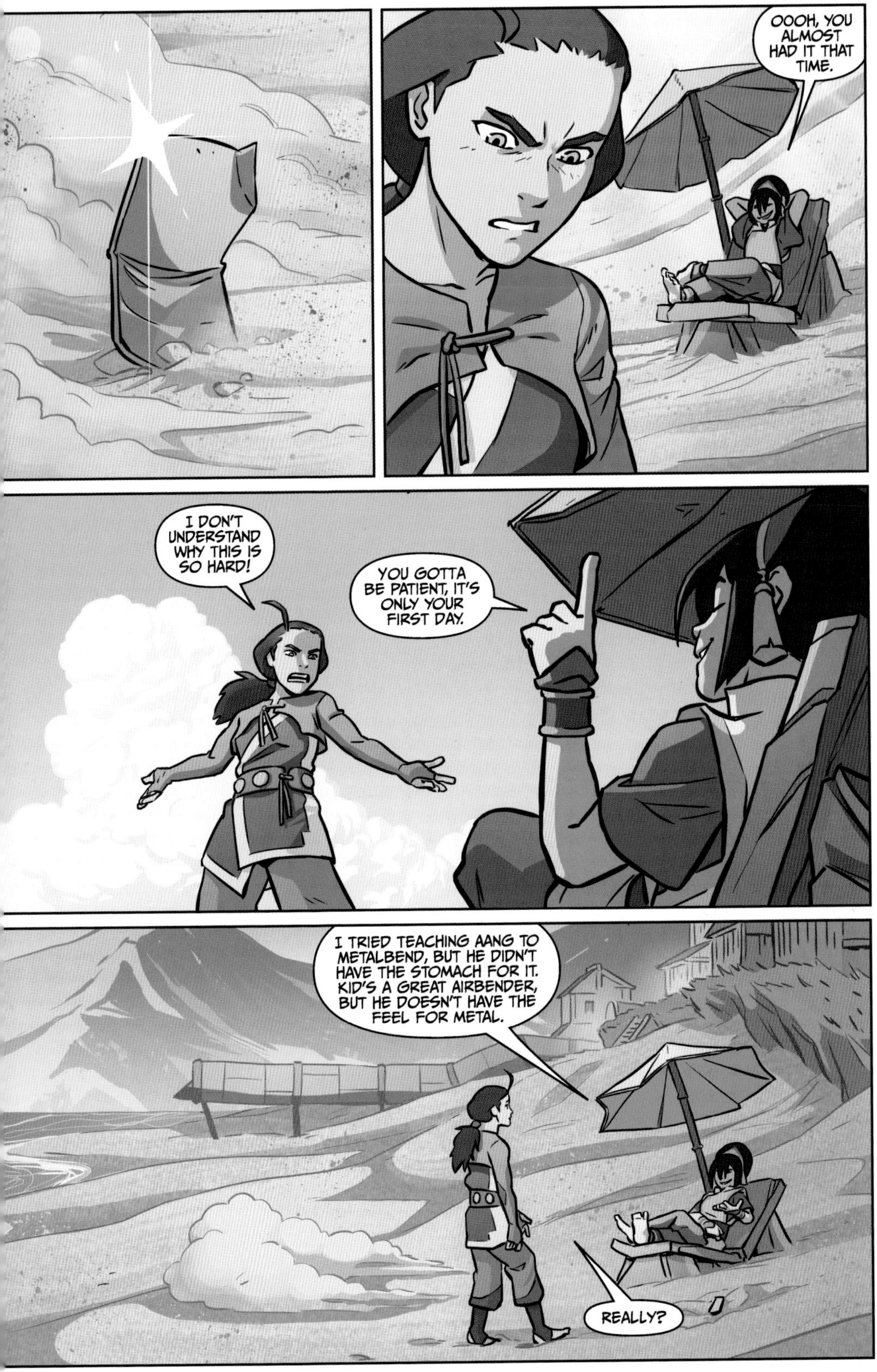
OOOH, YOU ALMOST HAD IT THAT TIME.
I DON'T UNDERSTAND WHY THIS IS SO HARD!
YOU GOTTA BE PATIENT, IT'S ONLY YOUR FIRST DAY.
I TRIED TEACHING AANG TO METALBEND, BUT HE DIDN'T HAVE THE STOMACH FOR IT. KID'S A GREAT AIRBENDER, BUT HE DOESN'T HAVE THE FEEL FOR METAL.
REALLY?

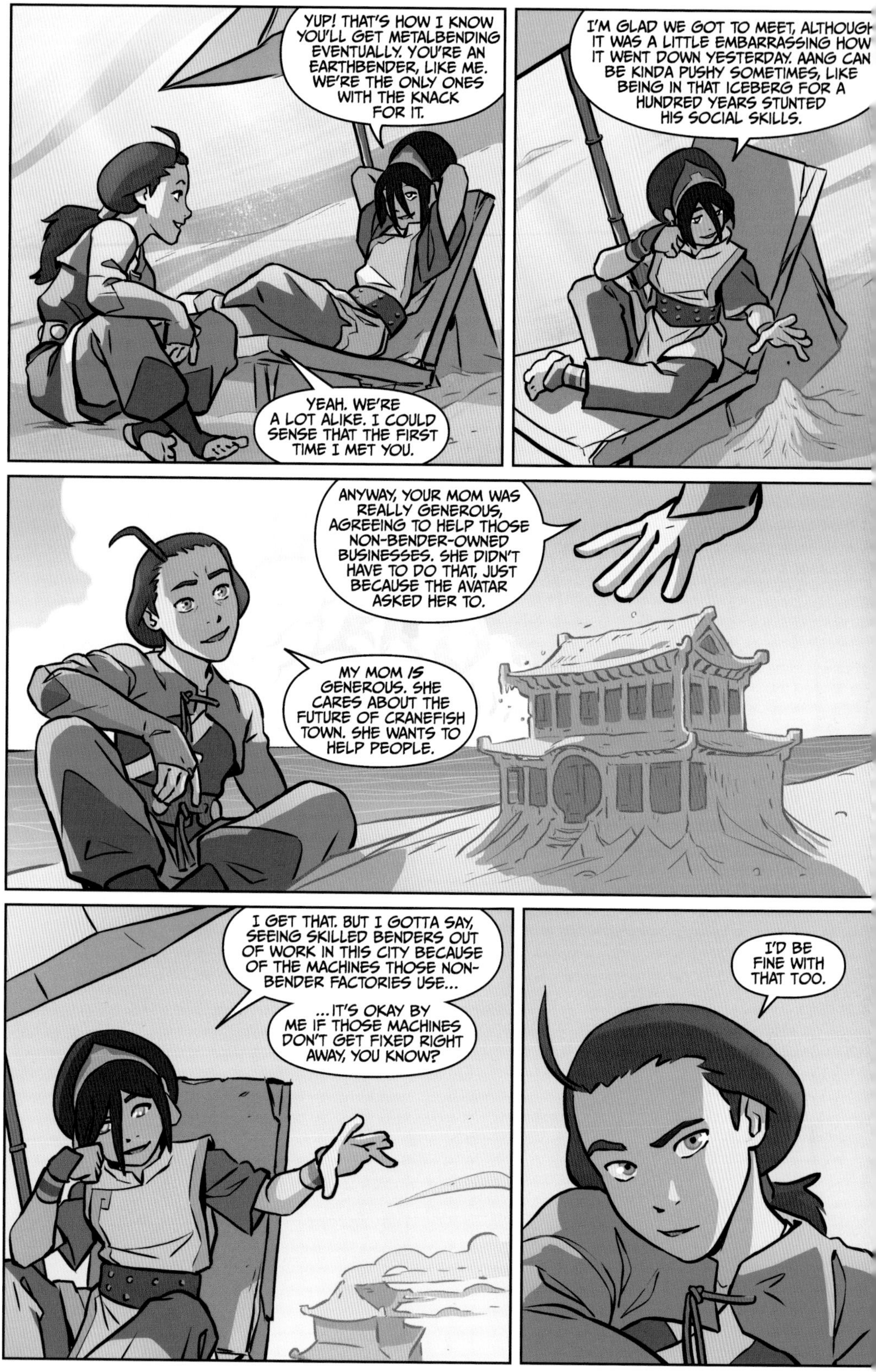
YUP! THAT'S HOW I KNOW YOU'LL GET METALBENDING EVENTUALLY. YOU'RE AN EARTHBENDER, LIKE ME. WE'RE THE ONLY ONES WITH THE KNACK FOR IT.
YEAH. WE'RE A LOT ALIKE. I COULD SENSE THAT THE FIRST TIME I MET YOU.
I'M GLAD WE GOT TO MEET, ALTHOUGH IT WAS A LITTLE EMBARRASSING HOW IT WENT DOWN YESTERDAY. AANG CAN BE KINDA PUSHY SOMETIMES, LIKE BEING IN THAT ICEBERG FOR A HUNDRED YEARS STUNTED HIS SOCIAL SKILLS.
ANYWAY, YOUR MOM WAS REALLY GENEROUS, AGREEING TO HELP THOSE NON-BENDER-OWNED BUSINESSES. SHE DIDN'T HAVE TO DO THAT, JUST BECAUSE THE AVATAR ASKED HER TO.
MY MOM IS GENEROUS. SHE CARES ABOUT THE FUTURE OF CRANEFISH TOWN. SHE WANTS TO HELP PEOPLE.
I GET THAT. BUT I GOTTA SAY, SEEING SKILLED BENDERS OUT OF WORK IN THIS CITY BECAUSE OF THE MACHINES THOSE NON-BENDER FACTORIES USE...
...IT'S OKAY BY ME IF THOSE MACHINES DON'T GET FIXED RIGHT AWAY, YOU KNOW?
I'D BE FINE WITH THAT TOO.

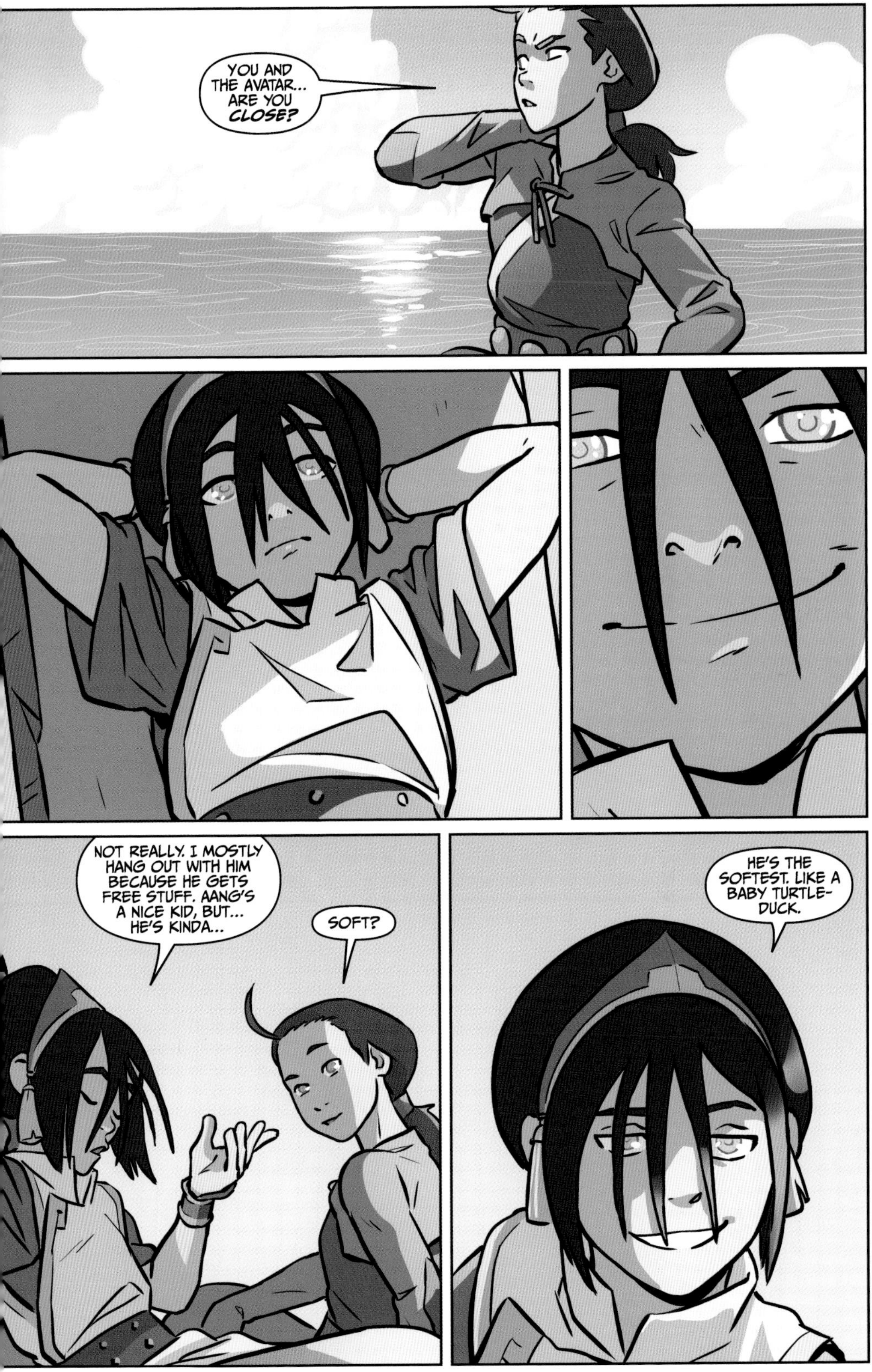
YOU AND THE AVATAR... ARE YOU *CLOSE?*
NOT REALLY. I MOSTLY HANG OUT WITH HIM BECAUSE HE GETS FREE STUFF. AANG'S A NICE KID, BUT... HE'S KINDA...
SOFT?
HE'S THE SOFTEST. LIKE A BABY TURTLE-DUCK.

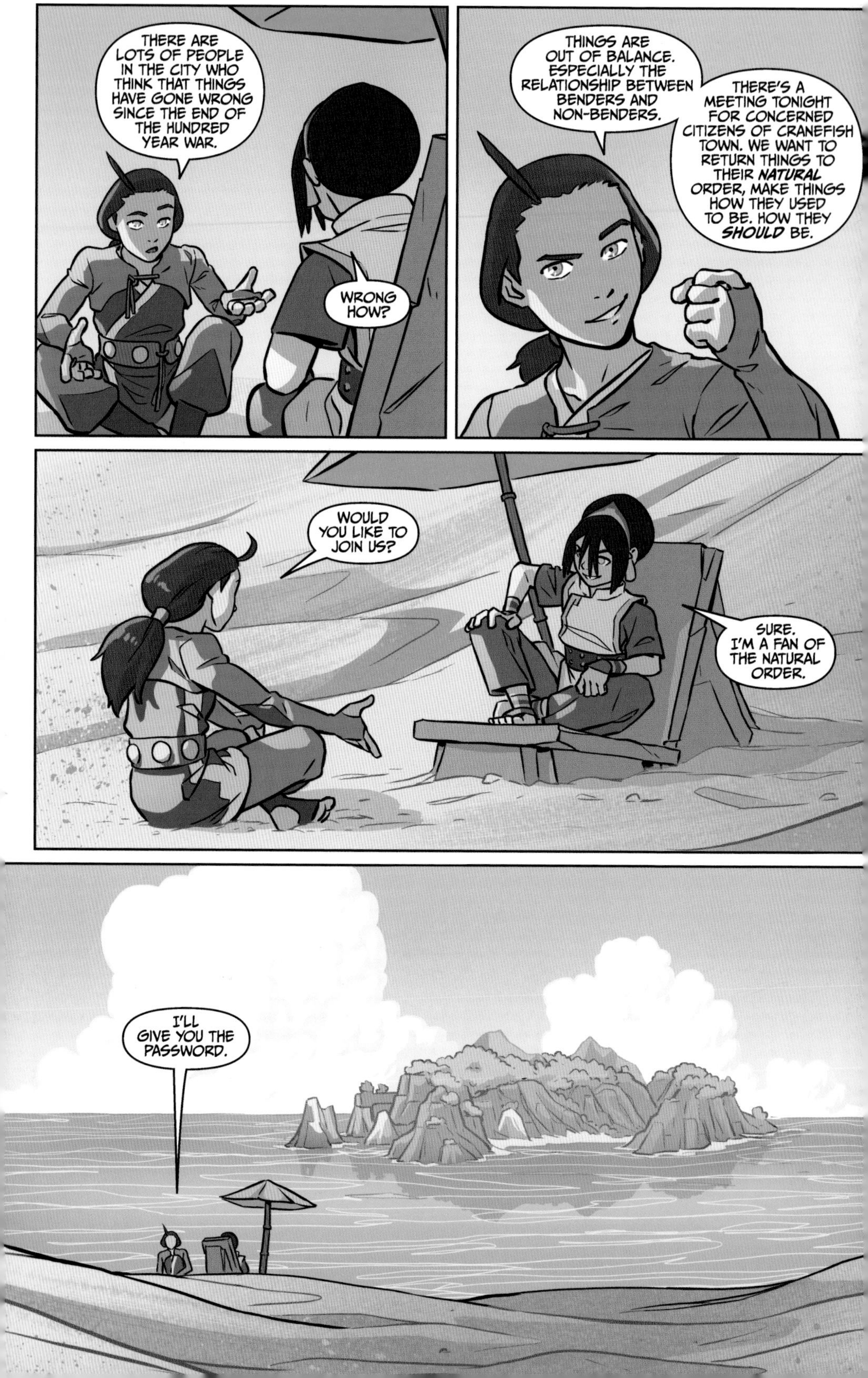
THERE ARE LOTS OF PEOPLE IN THE CITY WHO THINK THAT THINGS HAVE GONE WRONG SINCE THE END OF THE HUNDRED YEAR WAR.
WRONG HOW?
THINGS ARE OUT OF BALANCE. ESPECIALLY THE RELATIONSHIP BETWEEN BENDERS AND NON-BENDERS.
THERE'S A MEETING TONIGHT FOR CONCERNED CITIZENS OF CRANEFISH TOWN. WE WANT TO RETURN THINGS TO THEIR NATURAL ORDER, MAKE THINGS HOW THEY USED TO BE. HOW THEY SHOULD BE.
WOULD YOU LIKE TO JOIN US?
SURE. I'M A FAN OF THE NATURAL ORDER.
I'LL GIVE YOU THE PASSWORD.

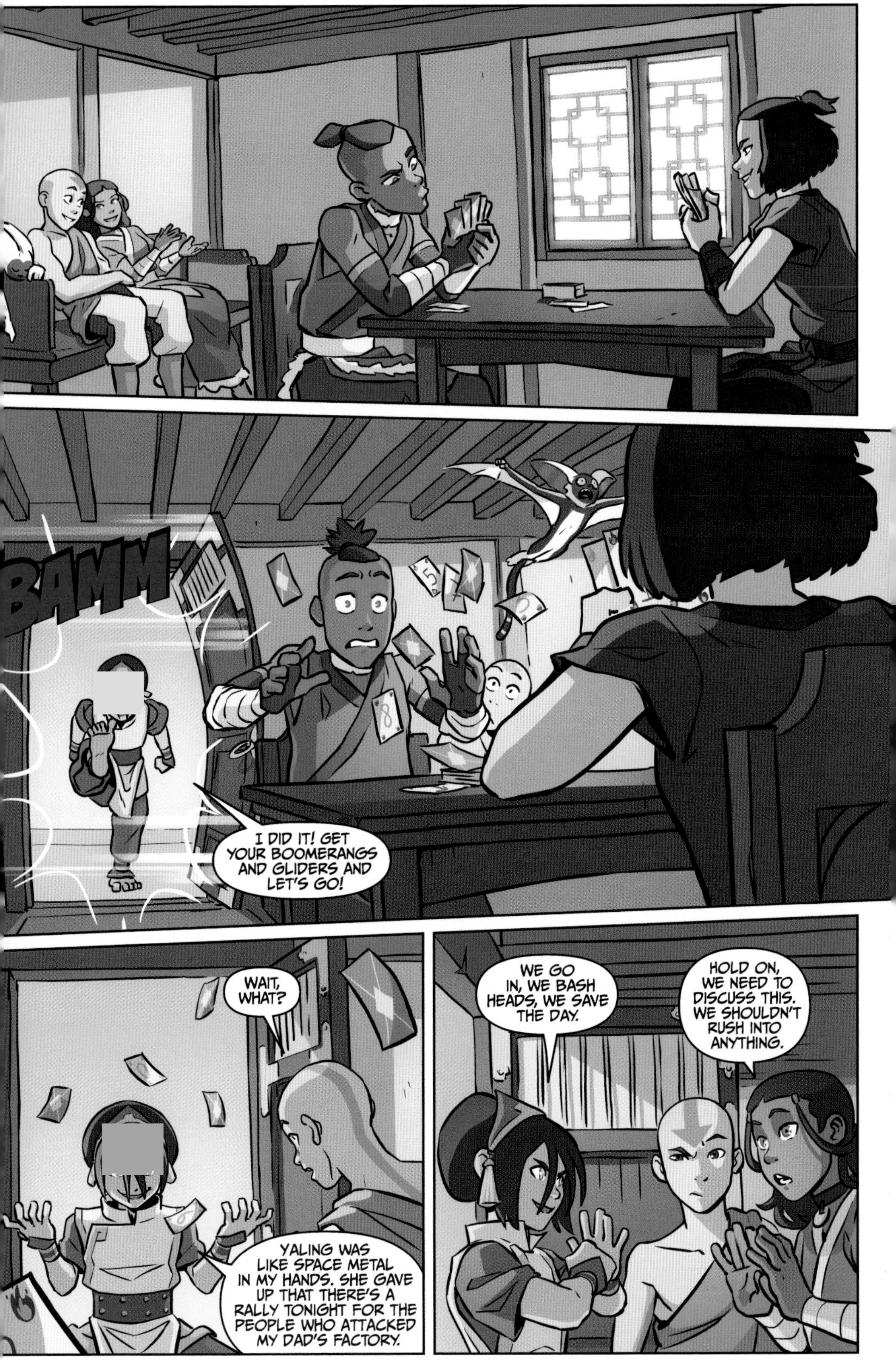
BAMM
I DID IT! GET YOUR BOOMERANGS AND GLIDERS AND LET'S GO!
WAIT, WHAT?
YALING WAS LIKE SPACE METAL IN MY HANDS. SHE GAVE UP THAT THERE'S A RALLY TONIGHT FOR THE PEOPLE WHO ATTACKED MY DAD'S FACTORY.
WE GO IN, WE BASH HEADS, WE SAVE THE DAY.
HOLD ON, WE NEED TO DISCUSS THIS. WE SHOULDN'T RUSH INTO ANYTHING.

WHAT'S TO DISCUSS?

WE DON'T KNOW WHY THE FACTORIES WERE ATTACKED, OR WHAT LILING'S INVOLVEMENT IS. SHE'S ON CRANEFISH TOWN'S BUSINESS COUNCIL. WE CAN'T ARREST HER WITHOUT PROOF SHE DID SOMETHING WRONG.

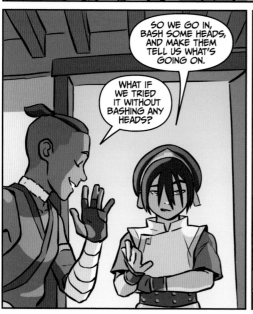

SO WE GO IN, BASH SOME HEADS, AND MAKE THEM TELL US WHAT'S GOING ON.

WHAT IF WE TRIED IT WITHOUT BASHING ANY HEADS?

WE *COULD* DO THAT, BUT... *WHY?*

WHAT ABOUT THIS. TOPH GOES TO THE MEETING WITH YALING, AND THE REST OF US DISGUISE OURSELVES AND SNEAK IN AFTER HER. THEN WE CAN GATHER INFORMATION.

SEEMS LIKE LESS FUN, BUT IF THAT'S THE WAY YOU WANT TO PLAY IT.

I THINK IT'S A GOOD PLAN.

IT'S A *GREAT* PLAN. ALSO, IT MEANS--

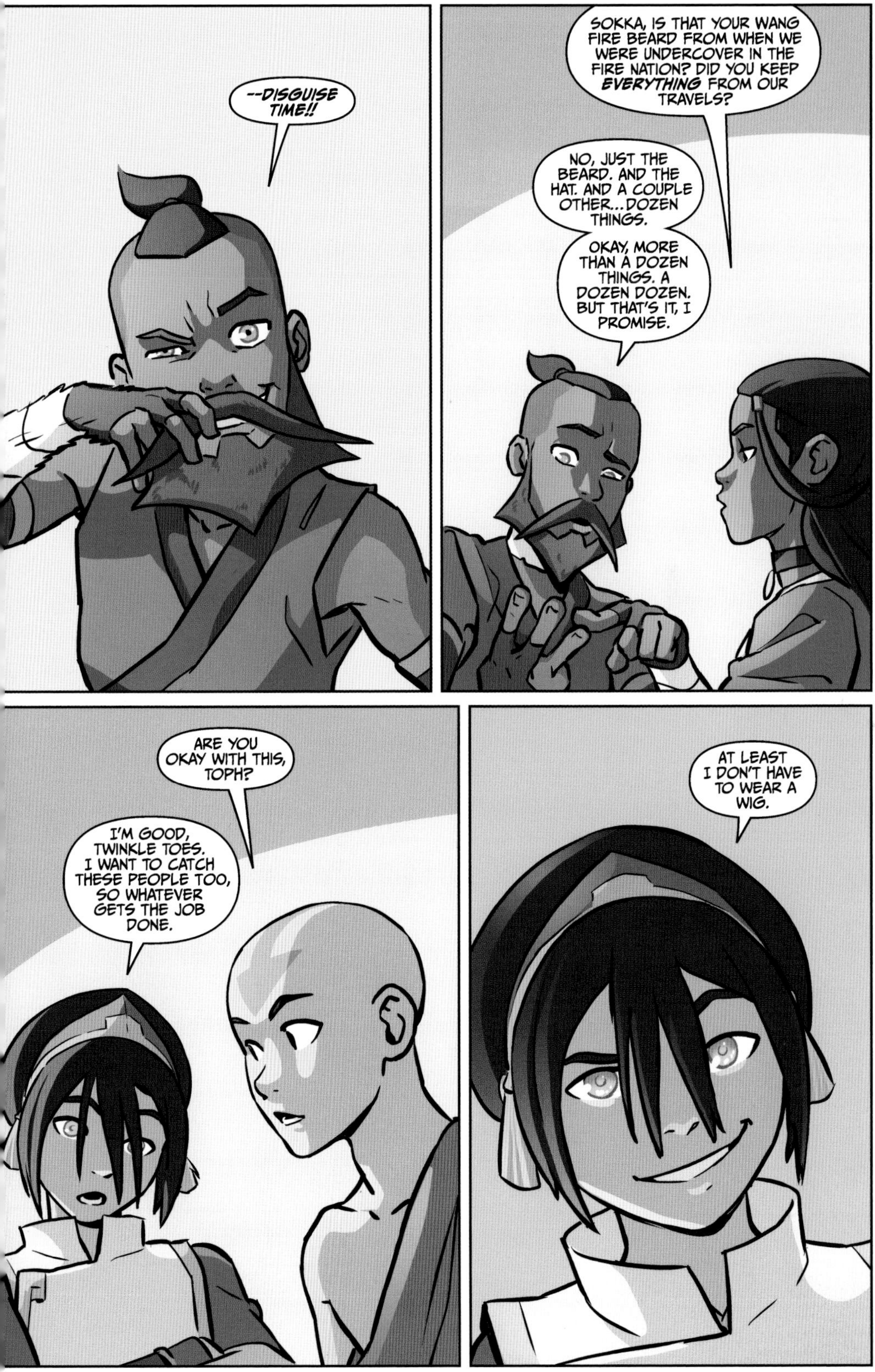
--DISGUISE TIME!!
SOKKA, IS THAT YOUR WANG FIRE BEARD FROM WHEN WE WERE UNDERCOVER IN THE FIRE NATION? DID YOU KEEP EVERYTHING FROM OUR TRAVELS?
NO, JUST THE BEARD. AND THE HAT. AND A COUPLE OTHER...DOZEN THINGS.
OKAY, MORE THAN A DOZEN THINGS. A DOZEN DOZEN. BUT THAT'S IT, I PROMISE.
ARE YOU OKAY WITH THIS, TOPH?
I'M GOOD, TWINKLE TOES. I WANT TO CATCH THESE PEOPLE TOO, SO WHATEVER GETS THE JOB DONE.
AT LEAST I DON'T HAVE TO WEAR A WIG.

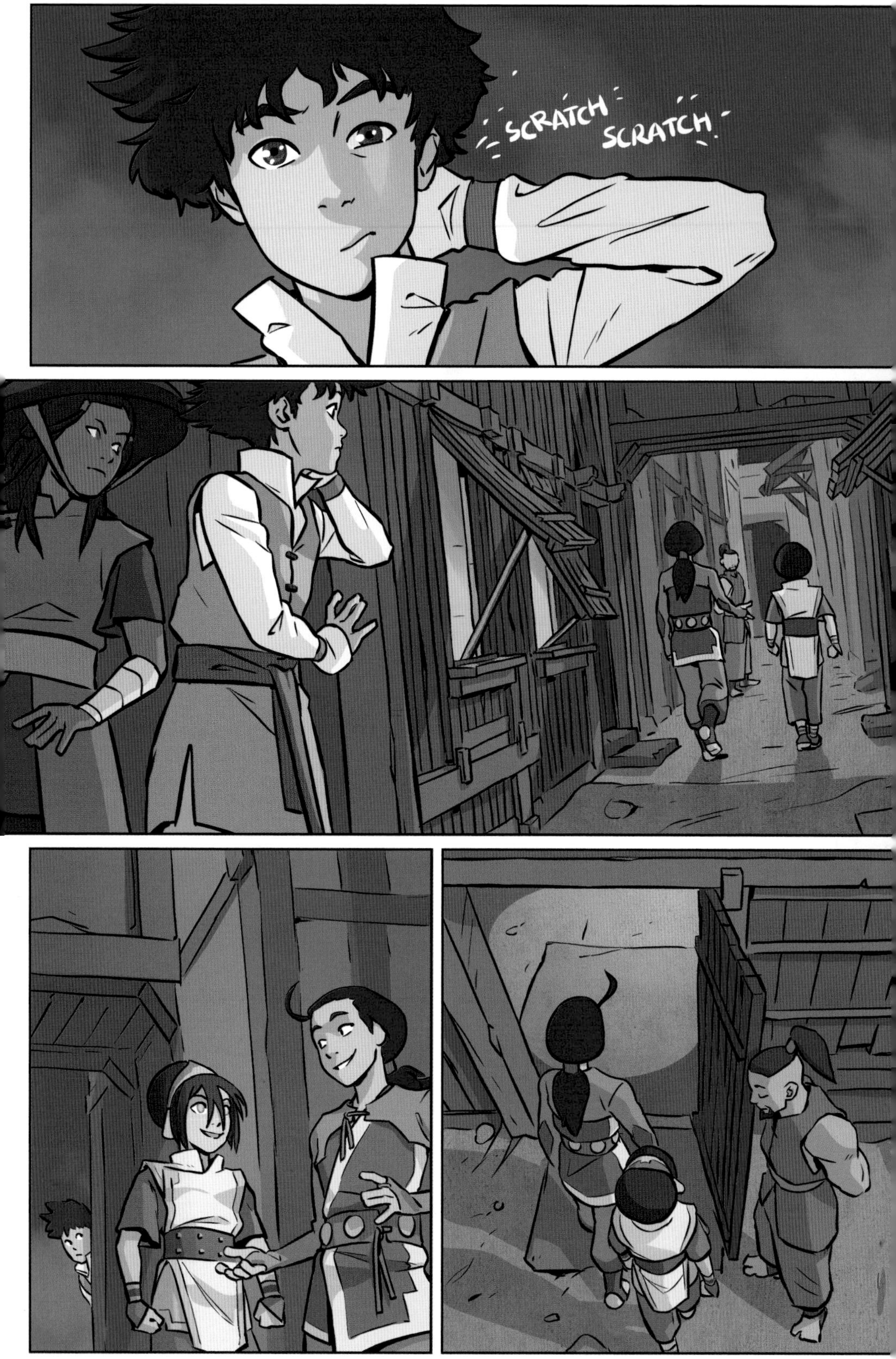
SCRATCH
SCRATCH

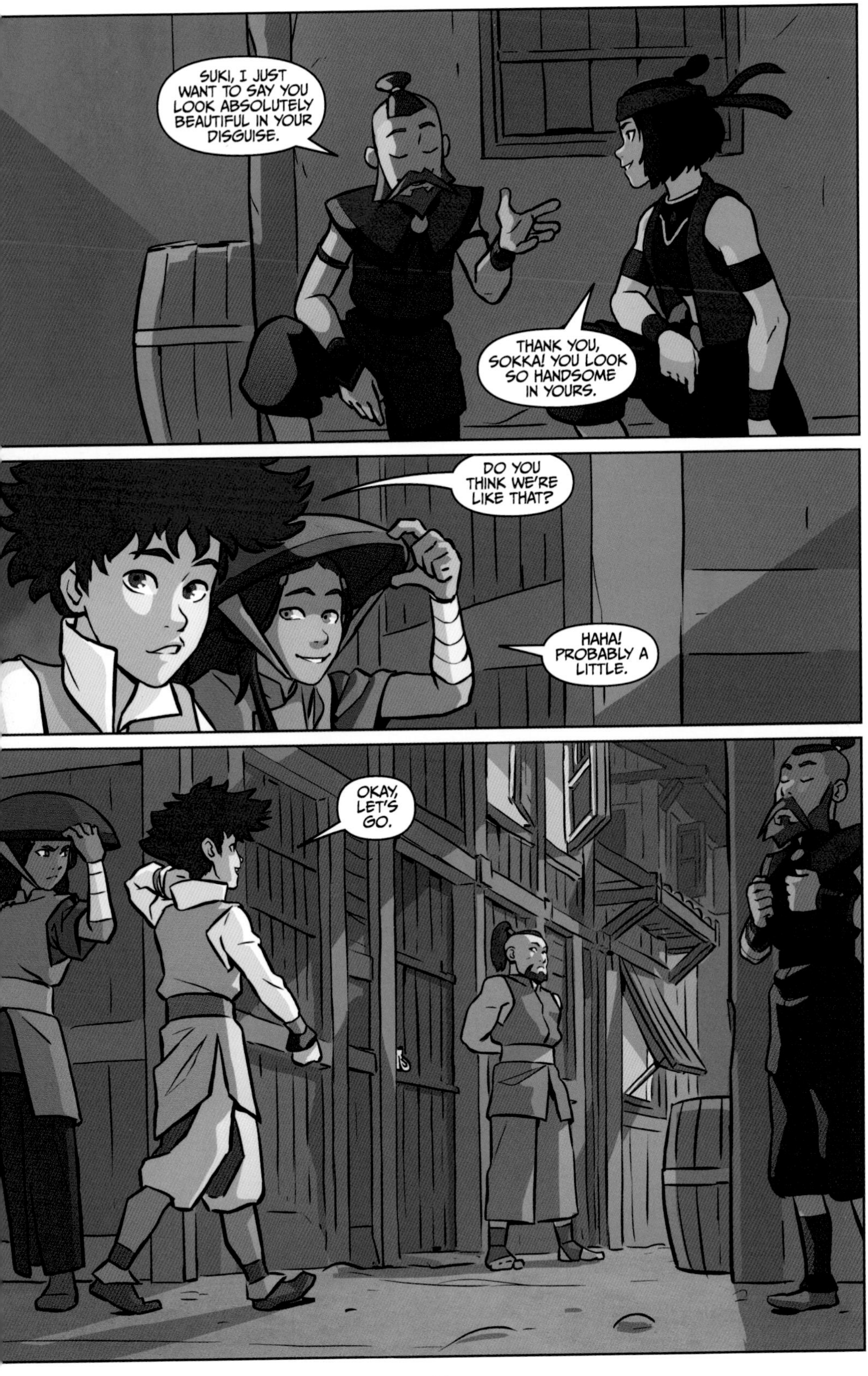
SUKI, I JUST WANT TO SAY YOU LOOK ABSOLUTELY BEAUTIFUL IN YOUR DISGUISE.
THANK YOU, SOKKA! YOU LOOK SO HANDSOME IN YOURS.
DO YOU THINK WE'RE LIKE THAT?
HAHA! PROBABLY A LITTLE.
OKAY, LET'S GO.

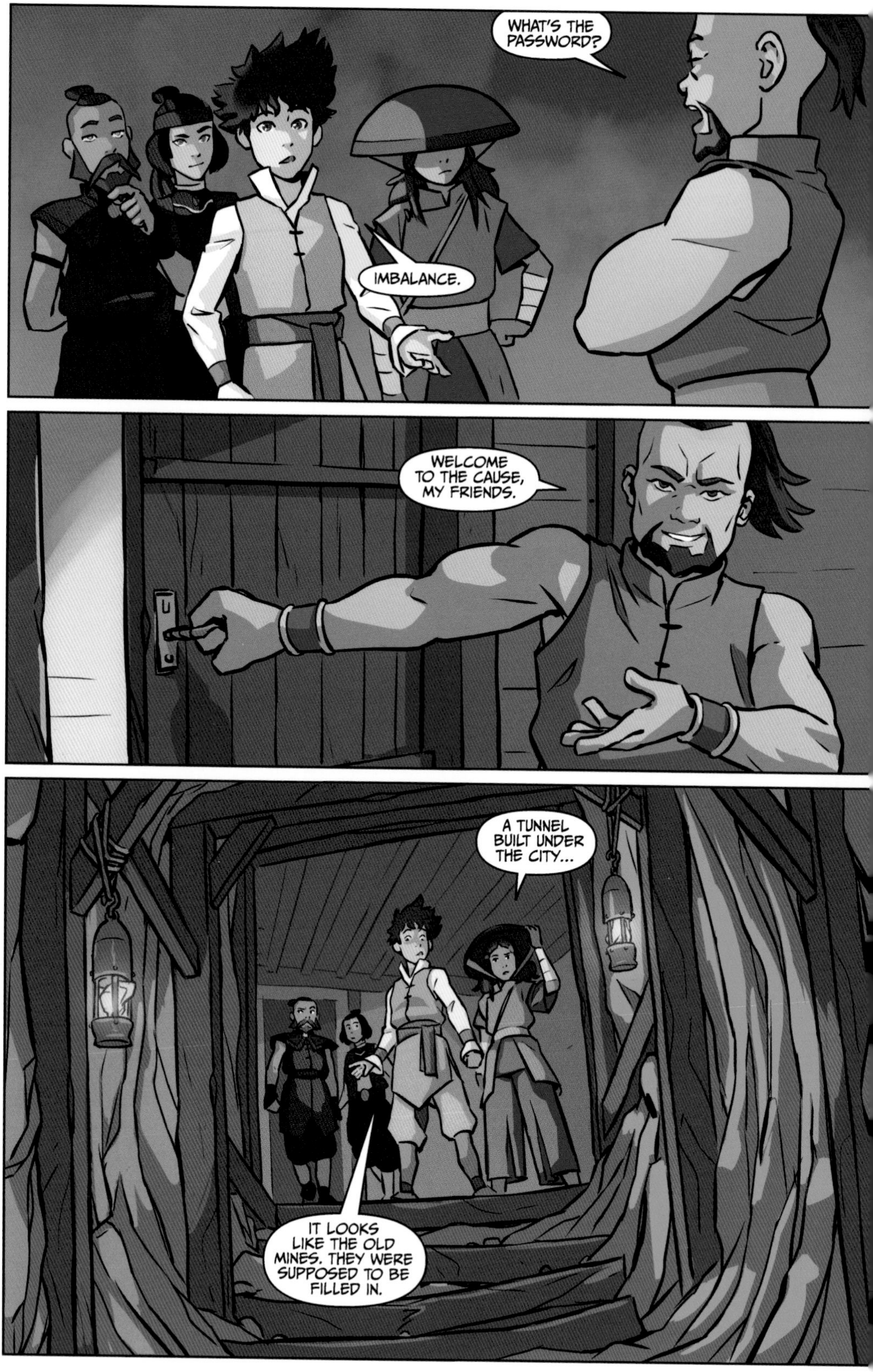
WHAT'S THE PASSWORD?
IMBALANCE.
WELCOME TO THE CAUSE, MY FRIENDS.
A TUNNEL BUILT UNDER THE CITY...
IT LOOKS LIKE THE OLD MINES. THEY WERE SUPPOSED TO BE FILLED IN.

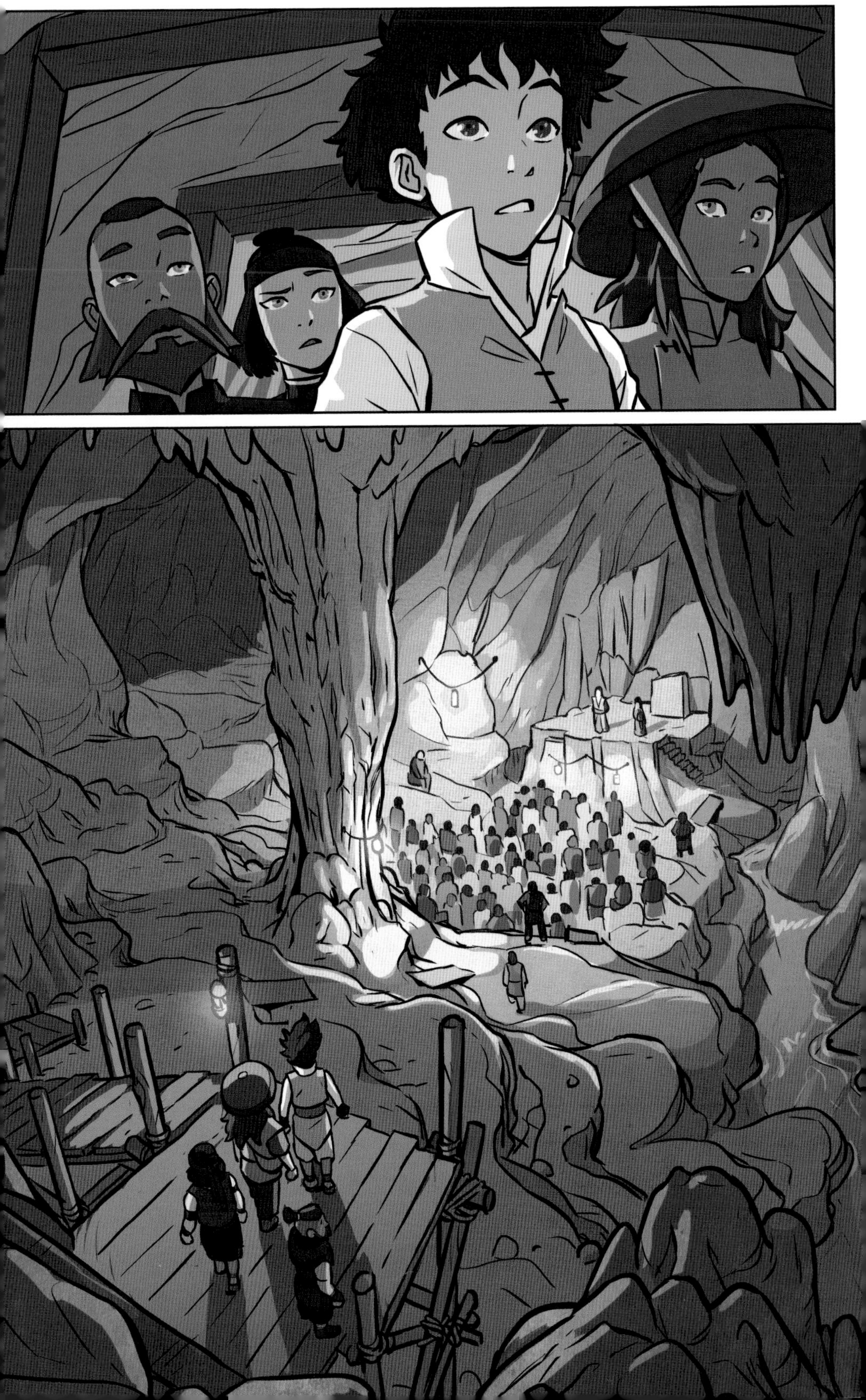

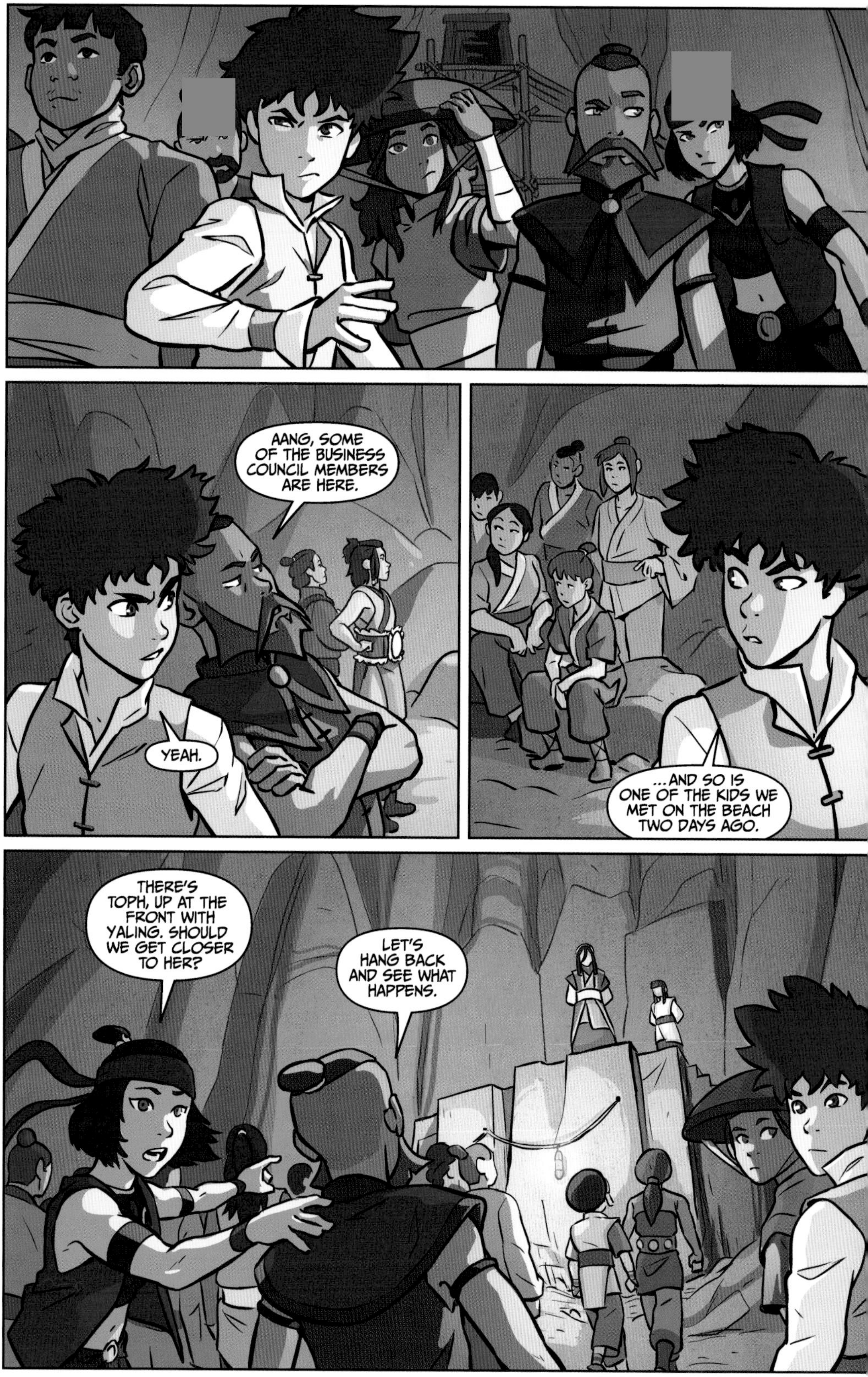
AANG, SOME OF THE BUSINESS COUNCIL MEMBERS ARE HERE.
YEAH.
...AND SO IS ONE OF THE KIDS WE MET ON THE BEACH TWO DAYS AGO.
THERE'S TOPH, UP AT THE FRONT WITH YALING. SHOULD WE GET CLOSER TO HER?
LET'S HANG BACK AND SEE WHAT HAPPENS.

BUT SHE'S UP THERE ALONE, SHOULDN'T WE BE CLOSER TO GIVE BACKUP--

BENDERS OF CRANEFISH TOWN! THIS CITY HAS FALLEN OUT OF BALANCE!

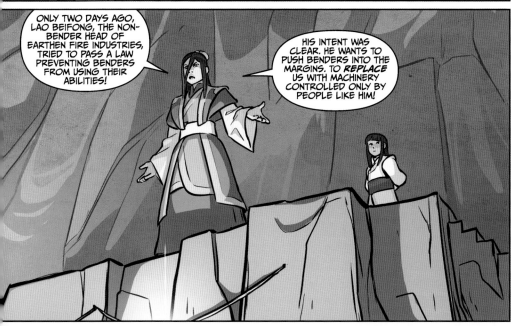

ONLY TWO DAYS AGO, LAO BEIFONG, THE NON-BENDER HEAD OF EARTHEN FIRE INDUSTRIES, TRIED TO PASS A LAW PREVENTING BENDERS FROM USING THEIR ABILITIES!

HIS INTENT WAS CLEAR. HE WANTS TO PUSH BENDERS INTO THE MARGINS. TO *REPLACE* US WITH MACHINERY CONTROLLED ONLY BY PEOPLE LIKE HIM!

WE WILL NOT BE REPLACED!

NOT WITHOUT A FIGHT!

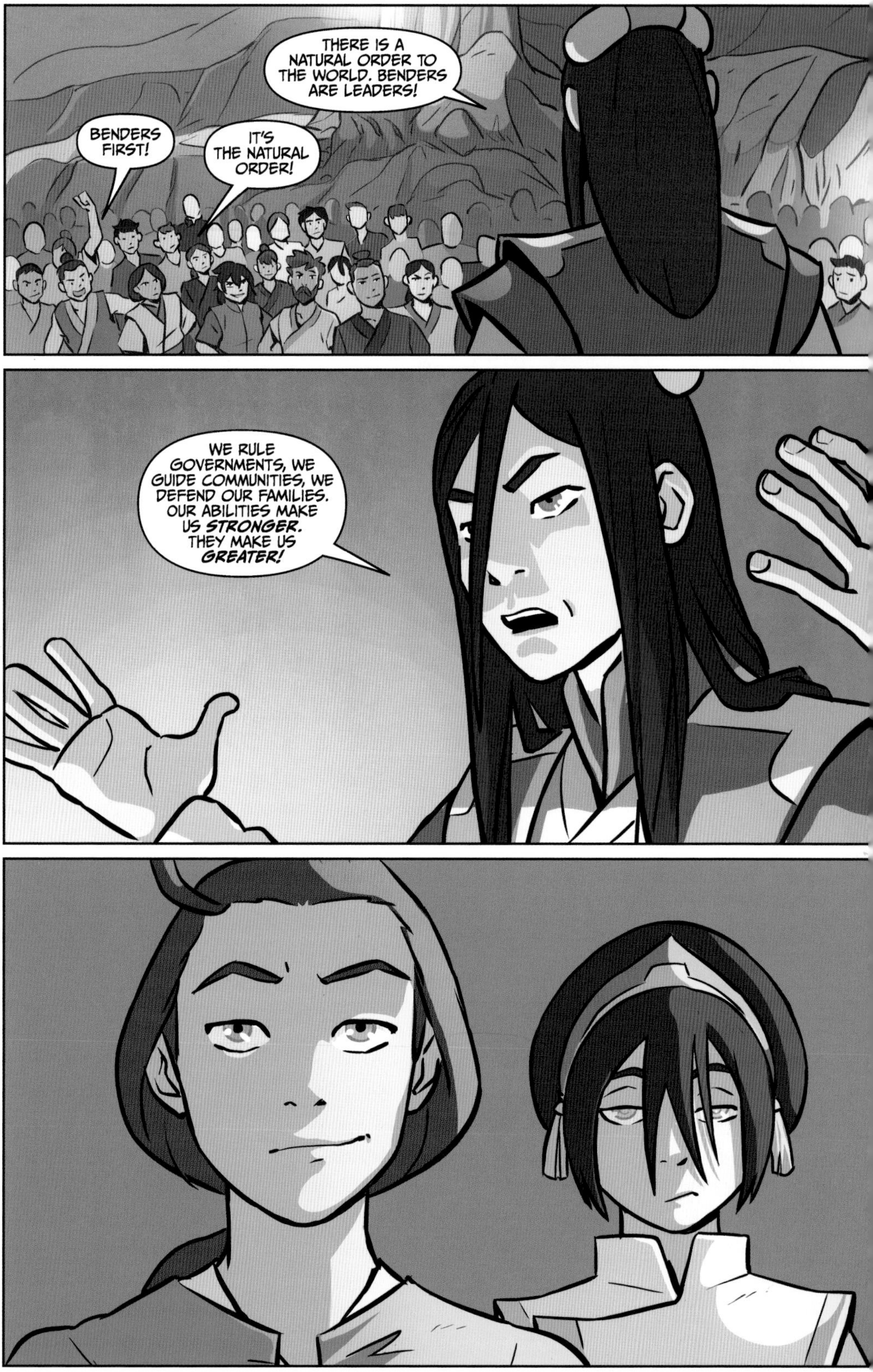

THERE IS A NATURAL ORDER TO THE WORLD. BENDERS ARE LEADERS!
BENDERS FIRST!
IT'S THE NATURAL ORDER!
WE RULE GOVERNMENTS, WE GUIDE COMMUNITIES, WE DEFEND OUR FAMILIES. OUR ABILITIES MAKE US ***STRONGER.*** THEY MAKE US ***GREATER!***

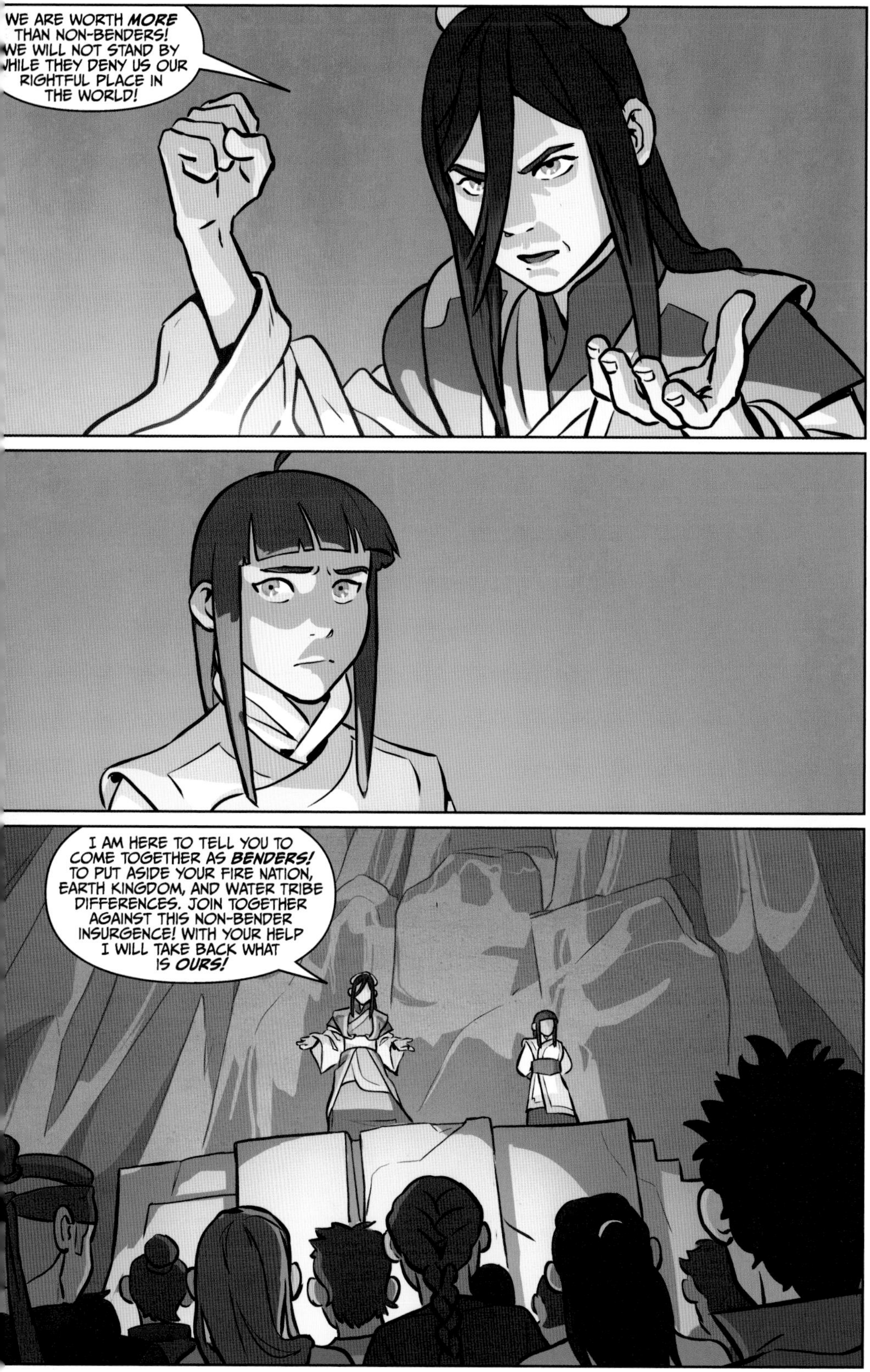
WE ARE WORTH ***MORE*** THAN NON-BENDERS! WE WILL NOT STAND BY WHILE THEY DENY US OUR RIGHTFUL PLACE IN THE WORLD!
I AM HERE TO TELL YOU TO COME TOGETHER AS ***BENDERS!*** TO PUT ASIDE YOUR FIRE NATION, EARTH KINGDOM, AND WATER TRIBE DIFFERENCES. JOIN TOGETHER AGAINST THIS NON-BENDER INSURGENCE! WITH YOUR HELP I WILL TAKE BACK WHAT IS ***OURS!***

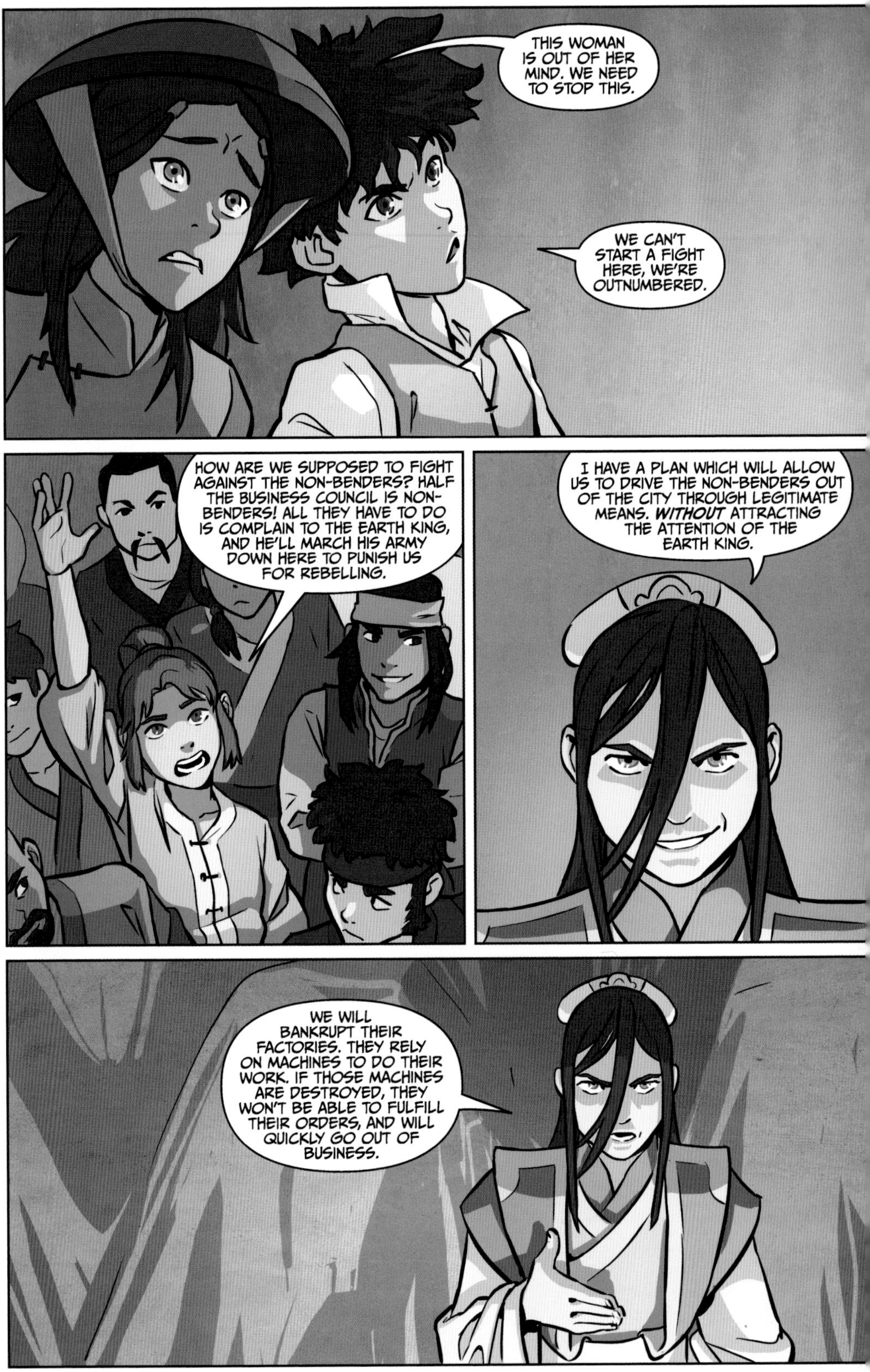
THIS WOMAN IS OUT OF HER MIND. WE NEED TO STOP THIS.
WE CAN'T START A FIGHT HERE, WE'RE OUTNUMBERED.
HOW ARE WE SUPPOSED TO FIGHT AGAINST THE NON-BENDERS? HALF THE BUSINESS COUNCIL IS NON-BENDERS! ALL THEY HAVE TO DO IS COMPLAIN TO THE EARTH KING, AND HE'LL MARCH HIS ARMY DOWN HERE TO PUNISH US FOR REBELLING.
I HAVE A PLAN WHICH WILL ALLOW US TO DRIVE THE NON-BENDERS OUT OF THE CITY THROUGH LEGITIMATE MEANS. WITHOUT ATTRACTING THE ATTENTION OF THE EARTH KING.
WE WILL BANKRUPT THEIR FACTORIES. THEY RELY ON MACHINES TO DO THEIR WORK. IF THOSE MACHINES ARE DESTROYED, THEY WON'T BE ABLE TO FULFILL THEIR ORDERS, AND WILL QUICKLY GO OUT OF BUSINESS.

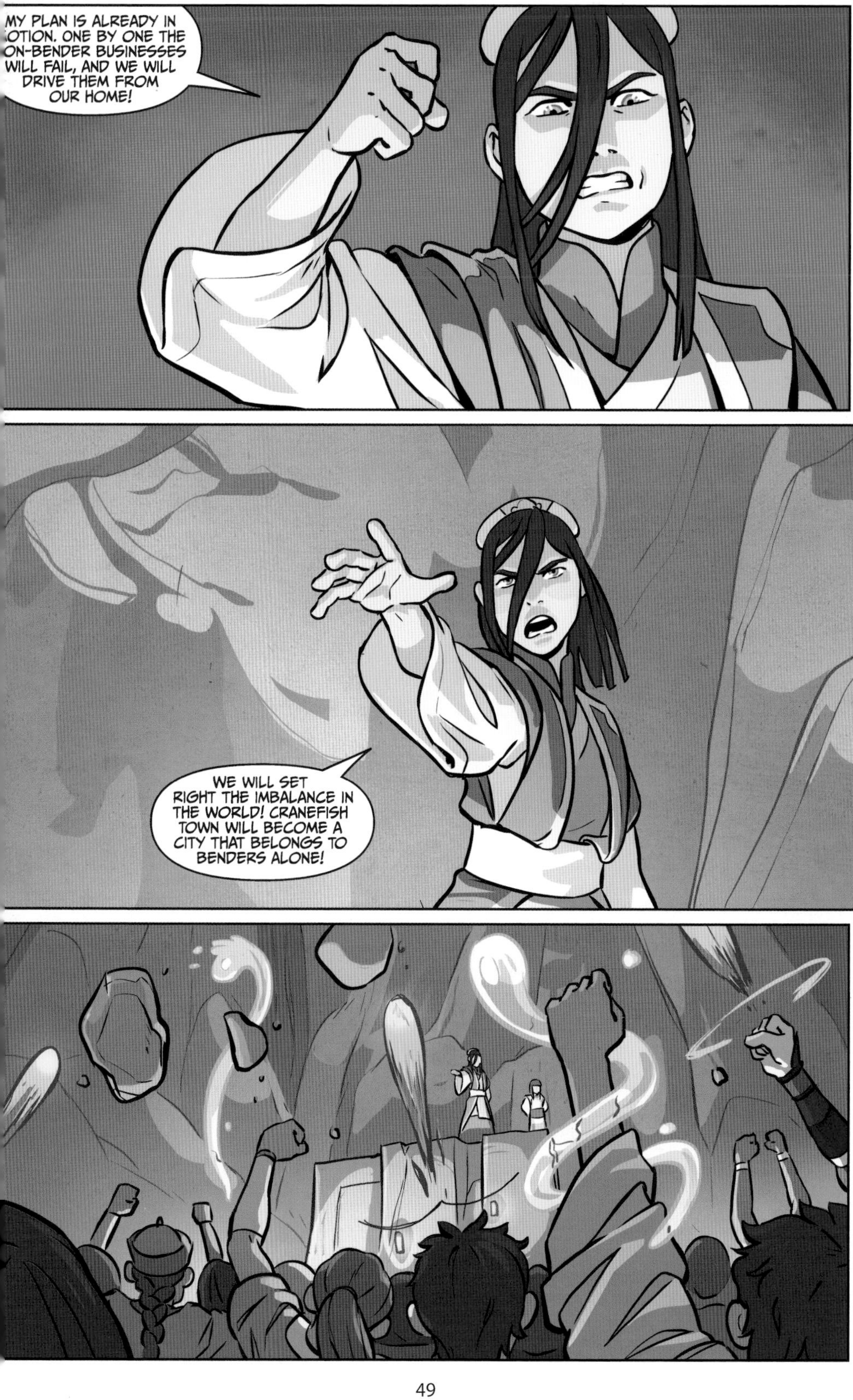
MY PLAN IS ALREADY IN OTION. ONE BY ONE THE ON-BENDER BUSINESSES WILL FAIL, AND WE WILL DRIVE THEM FROM OUR HOME!
WE WILL SET RIGHT THE IMBALANCE IN THE WORLD! CRANEFISH TOWN WILL BECOME A CITY THAT BELONGS TO BENDERS ALONE!

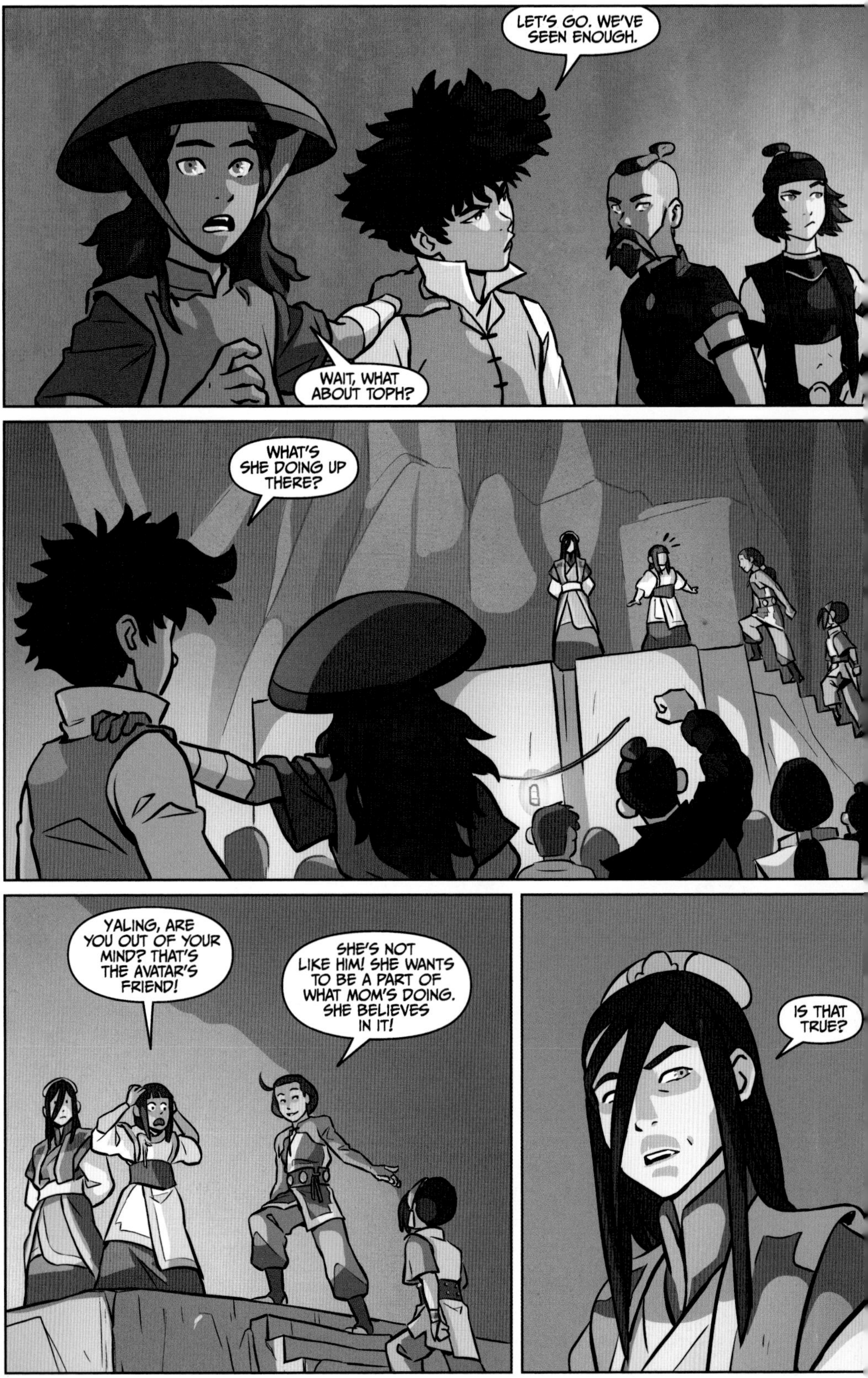
LET'S GO. WE'VE SEEN ENOUGH.
WAIT, WHAT ABOUT TOPH?
WHAT'S SHE DOING UP THERE?
YALING, ARE YOU OUT OF YOUR MIND? THAT'S THE AVATAR'S FRIEND!
SHE'S NOT LIKE HIM! SHE WANTS TO BE A PART OF WHAT MOM'S DOING. SHE BELIEVES IN IT!
IS THAT TRUE?

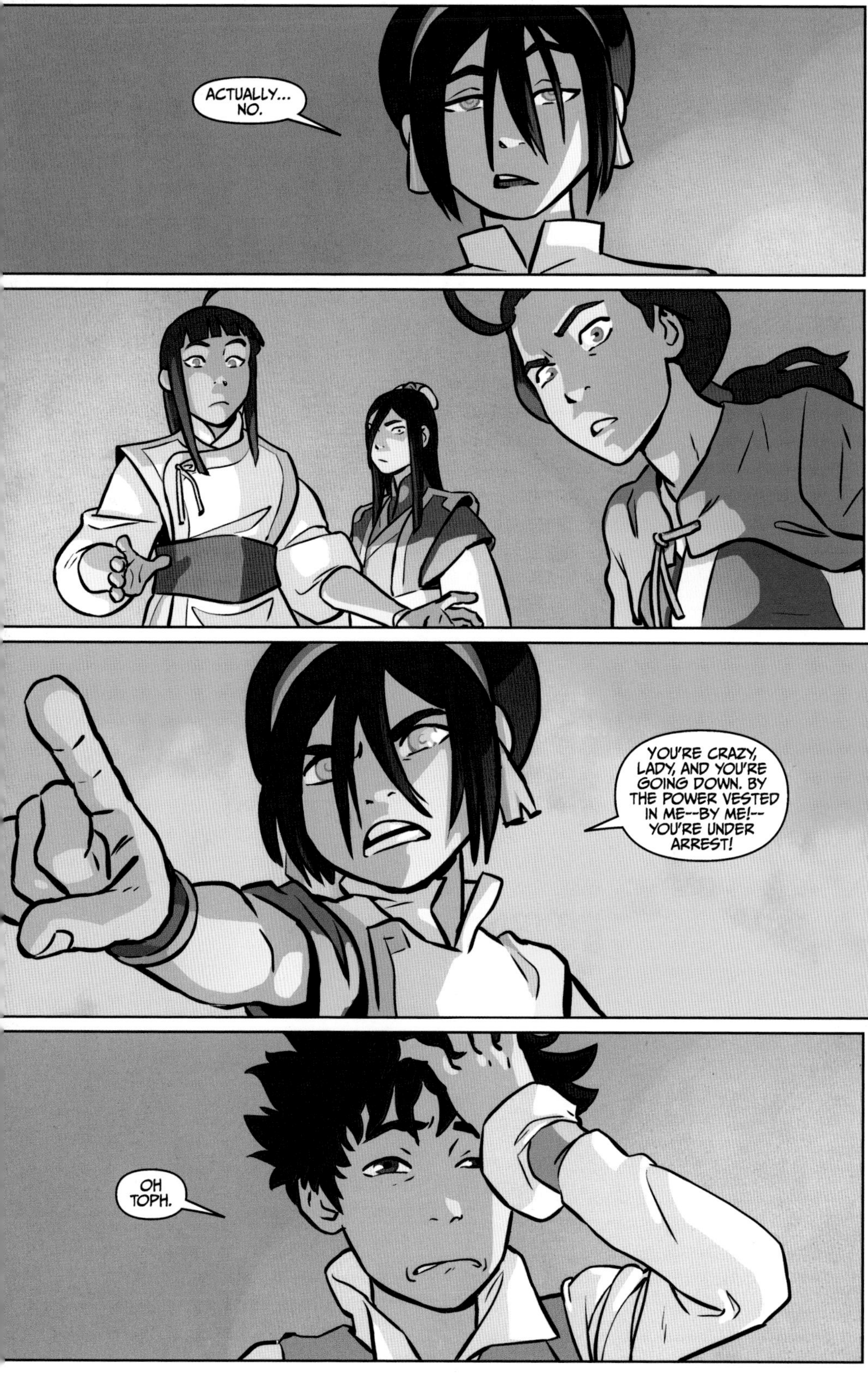
ACTUALLY... NO.
YOU'RE CRAZY, LADY, AND YOU'RE GOING DOWN. BY THE POWER VESTED IN ME--BY ME!-- YOU'RE UNDER ARREST!
OH TOPH.

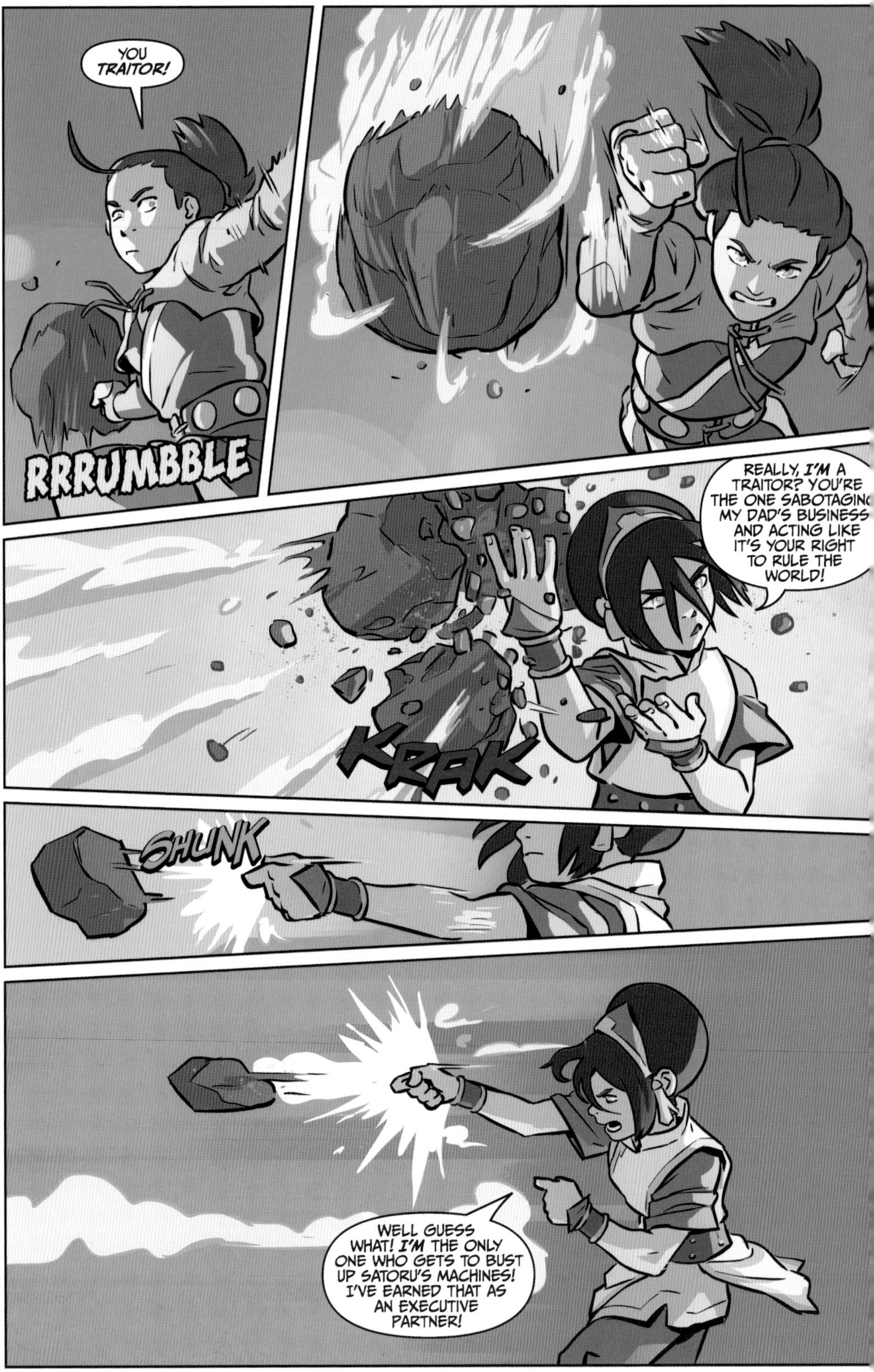
YOU TRAITOR!
RRRUMBBLE
REALLY, *I'M* A TRAITOR? YOU'RE THE ONE SABOTAGIN MY DAD'S BUSINESS AND ACTING LIKE IT'S YOUR RIGHT TO RULE THE WORLD!
KRAK
SHUNK
WELL GUESS WHAT! *I'M* THE ONLY ONE WHO GETS TO BUST UP SATORU'S MACHINES! I'VE EARNED THAT AS AN EXECUTIVE PARTNER!

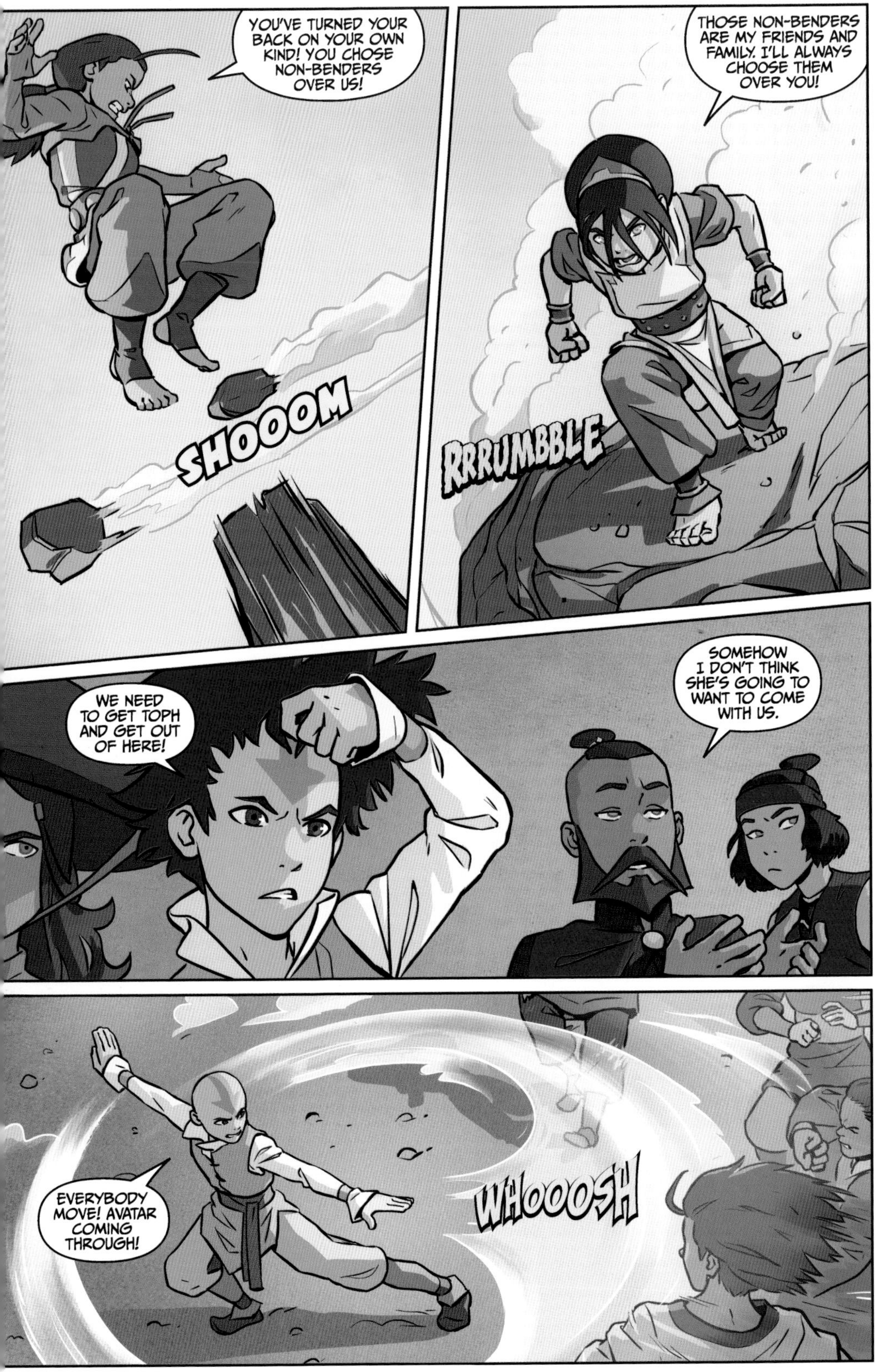
YOU'VE TURNED YOUR BACK ON YOUR OWN KIND! YOU CHOSE NON-BENDERS OVER US!
SHOOOM
THOSE NON-BENDERS ARE MY FRIENDS AND FAMILY. I'LL ALWAYS CHOOSE THEM OVER YOU!
RRRUMBBLE
WE NEED TO GET TOPH AND GET OUT OF HERE!
SOMEHOW I DON'T THINK SHE'S GOING TO WANT TO COME WITH US.
EVERYBODY MOVE! AVATAR COMING THROUGH!
WHOOOSH

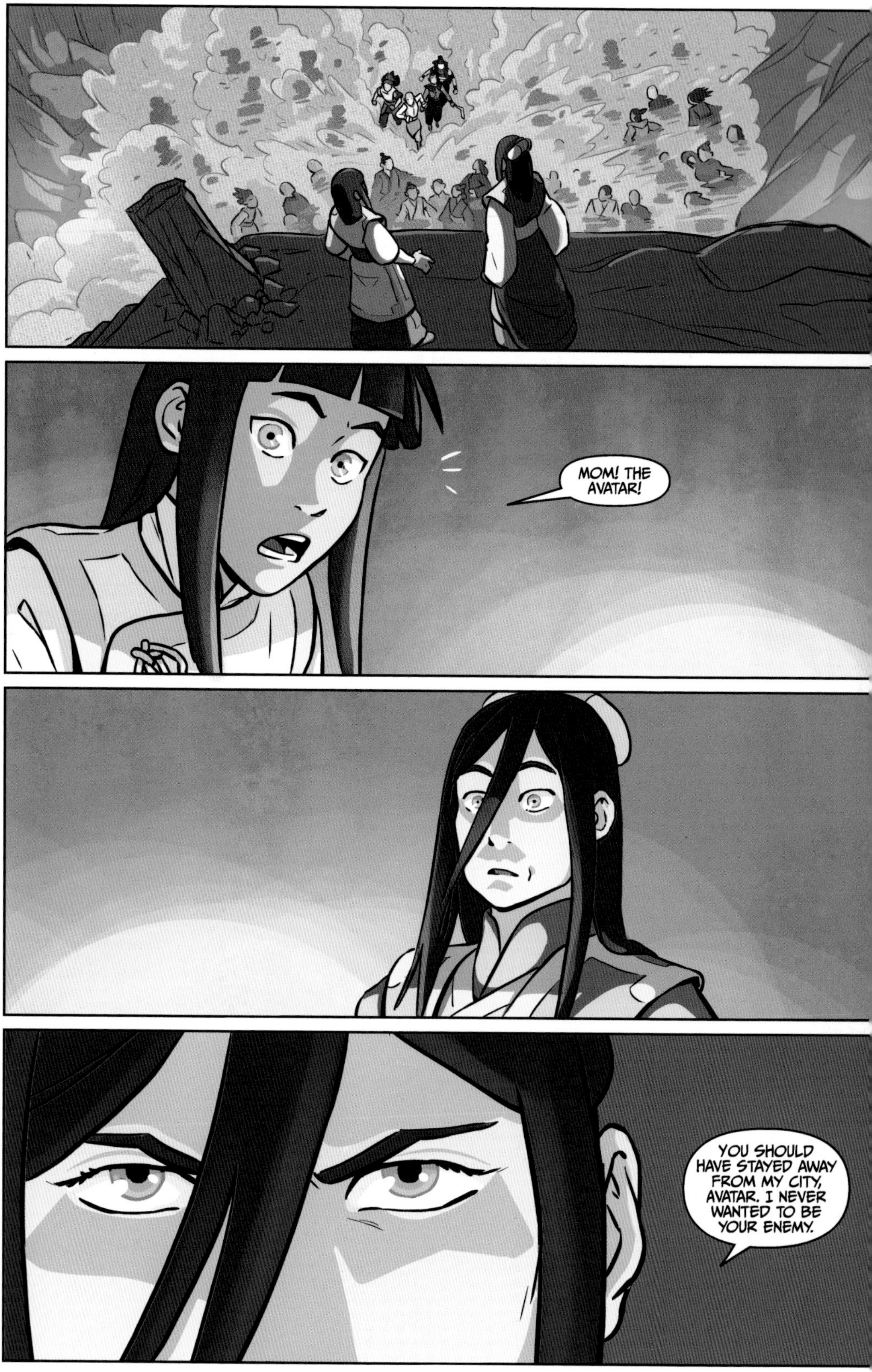

MOM! THE AVATAR!
YOU SHOULD HAVE STAYED AWAY FROM MY CITY, AVATAR. I NEVER WANTED TO BE YOUR ENEMY.

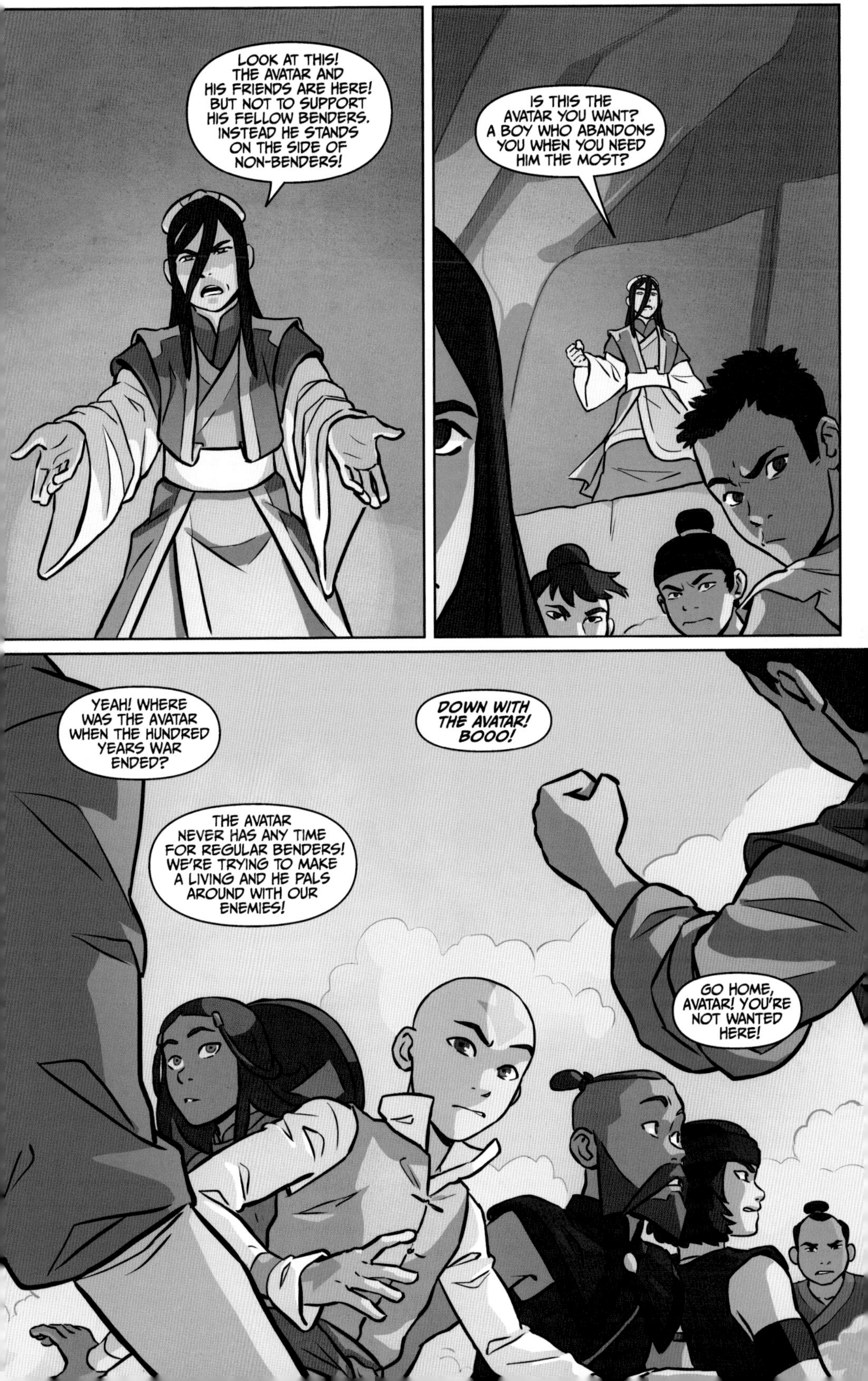
LOOK AT THIS! THE AVATAR AND HIS FRIENDS ARE HERE! BUT NOT TO SUPPORT HIS FELLOW BENDERS. INSTEAD HE STANDS ON THE SIDE OF NON-BENDERS!
IS THIS THE AVATAR YOU WANT? A BOY WHO ABANDONS YOU WHEN YOU NEED HIM THE MOST?
YEAH! WHERE WAS THE AVATAR WHEN THE HUNDRED YEARS WAR ENDED?
DOWN WITH THE AVATAR! BOOO!
THE AVATAR NEVER HAS ANY TIME FOR REGULAR BENDERS! WE'RE TRYING TO MAKE A LIVING AND HE PALS AROUND WITH OUR ENEMIES!
GO HOME, AVATAR! YOU'RE NOT WANTED HERE!

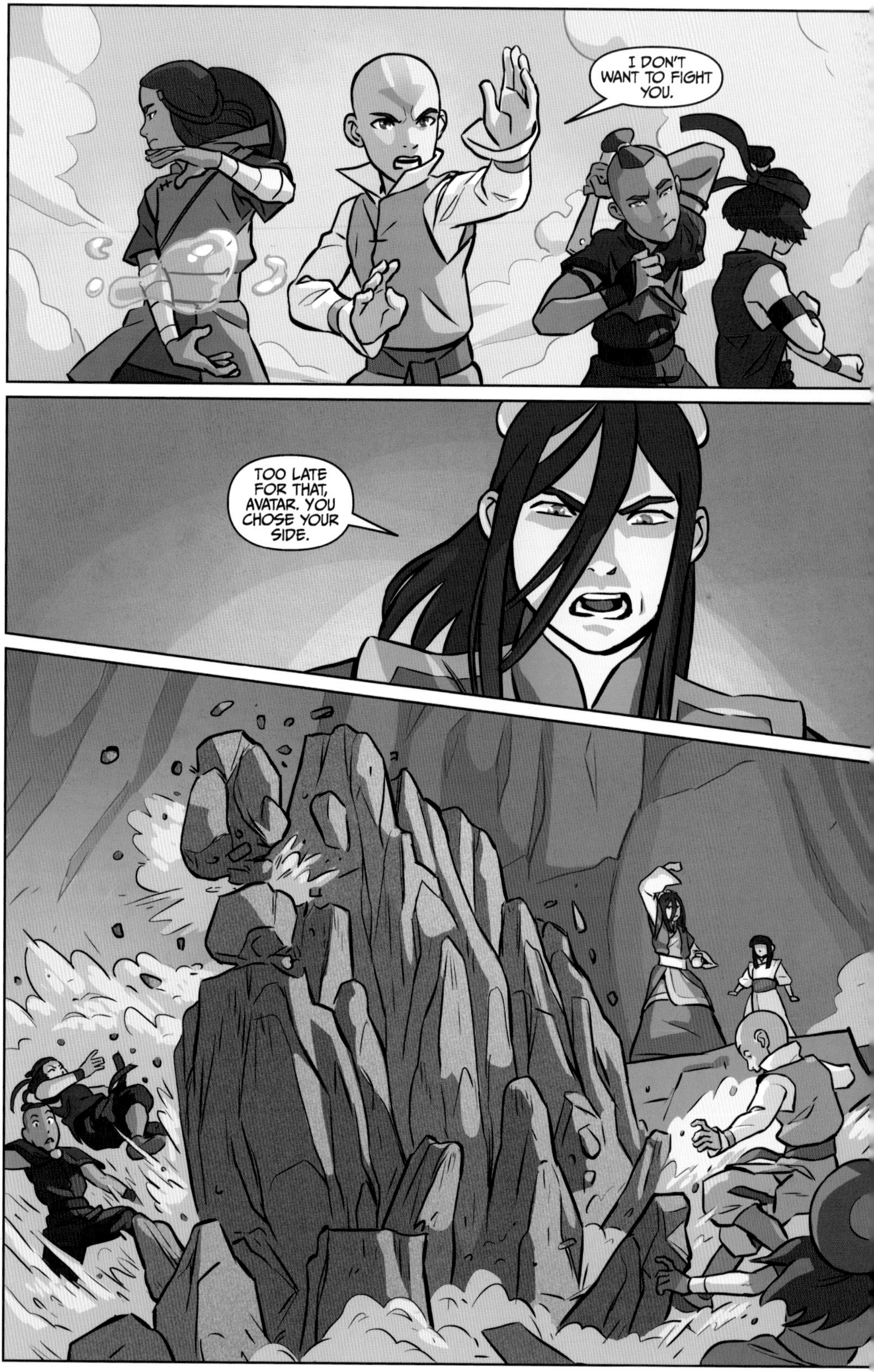
I DON'T WANT TO FIGHT YOU.
TOO LATE FOR THAT, AVATAR. YOU CHOSE YOUR SIDE.

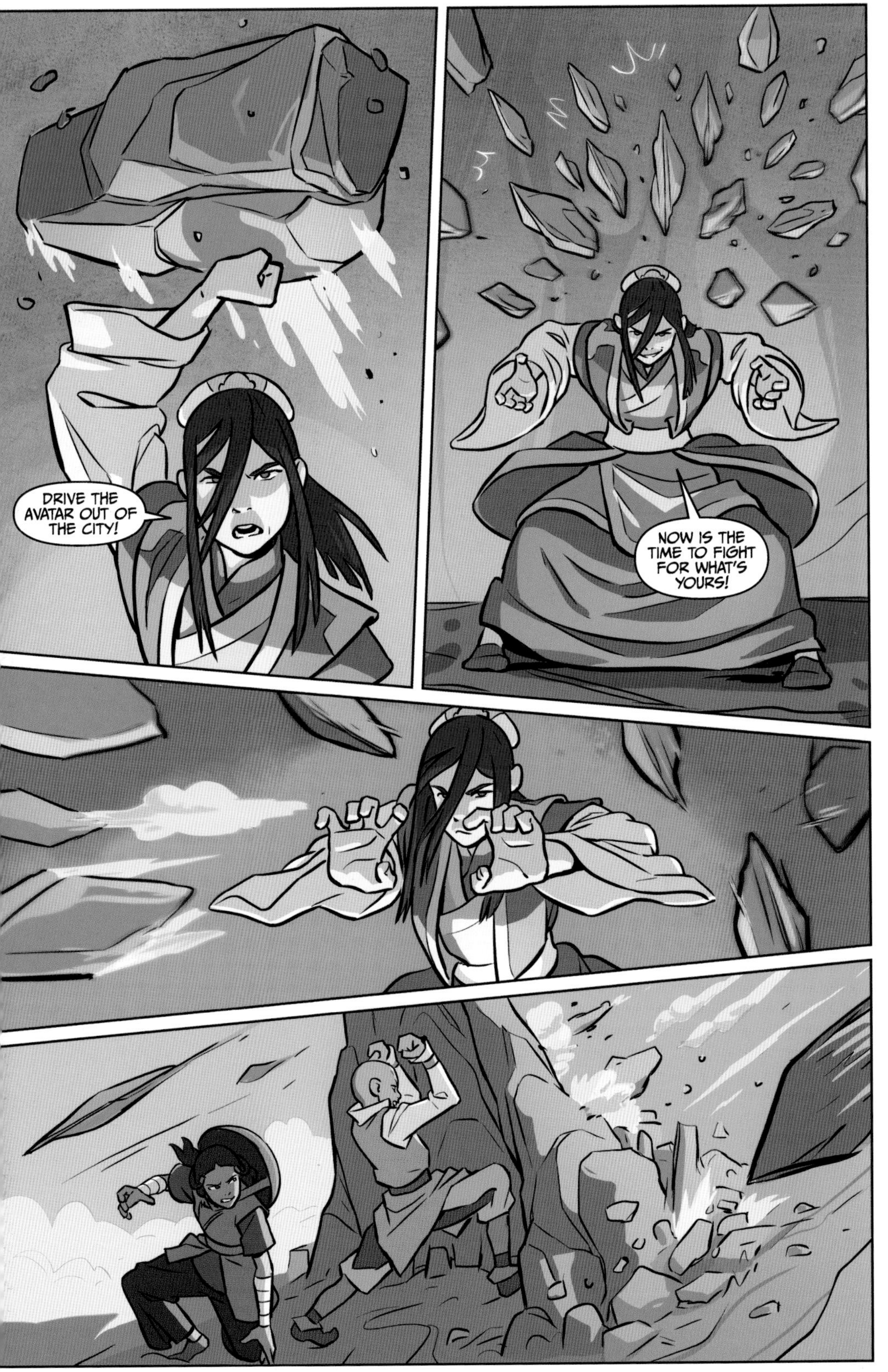
DRIVE THE AVATAR OUT OF THE CITY!
NOW IS THE TIME TO FIGHT FOR WHAT'S YOURS!

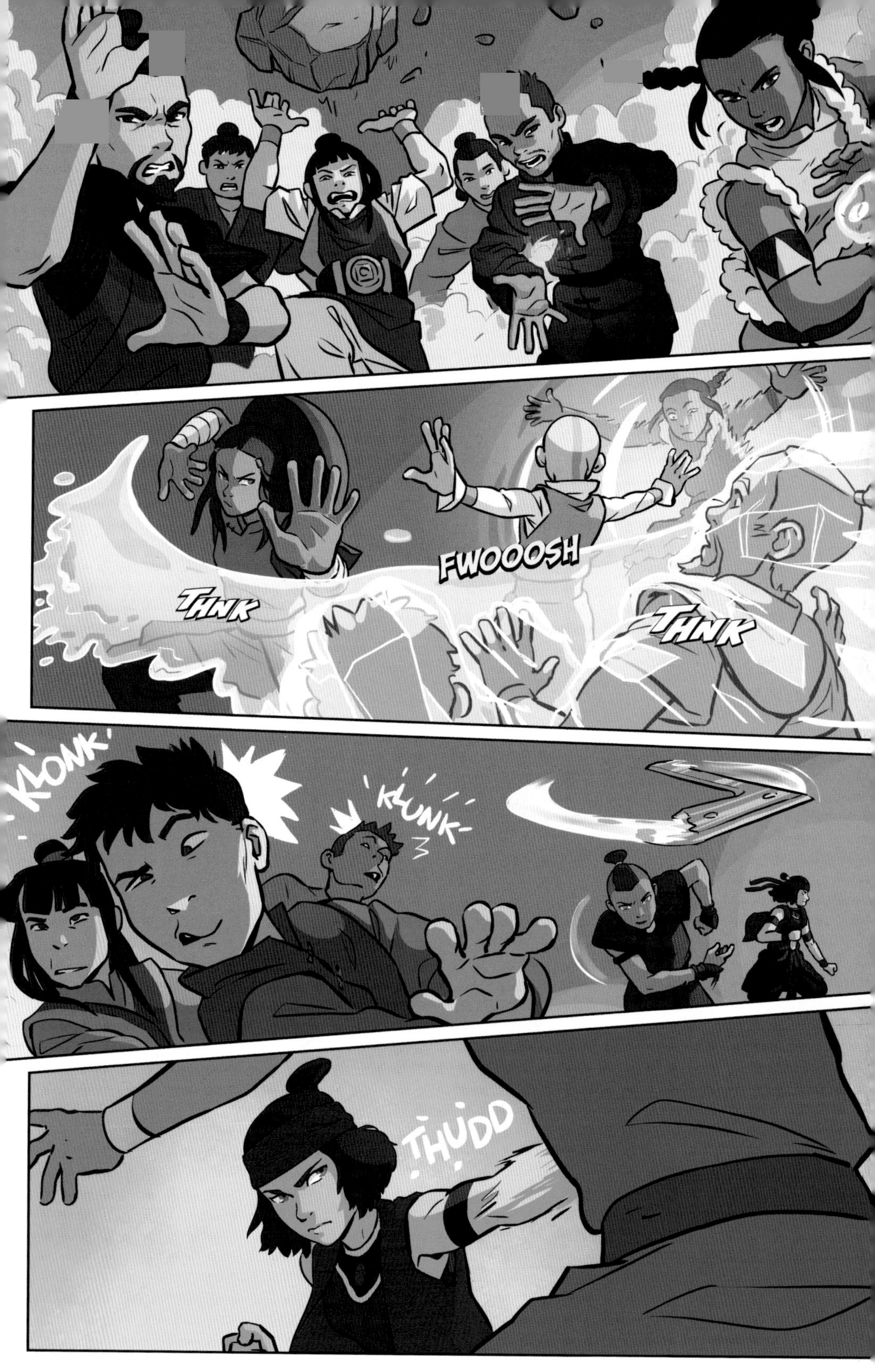
THNK
FWOOOSH
THNK
KLONK
KLUNK
THUDD

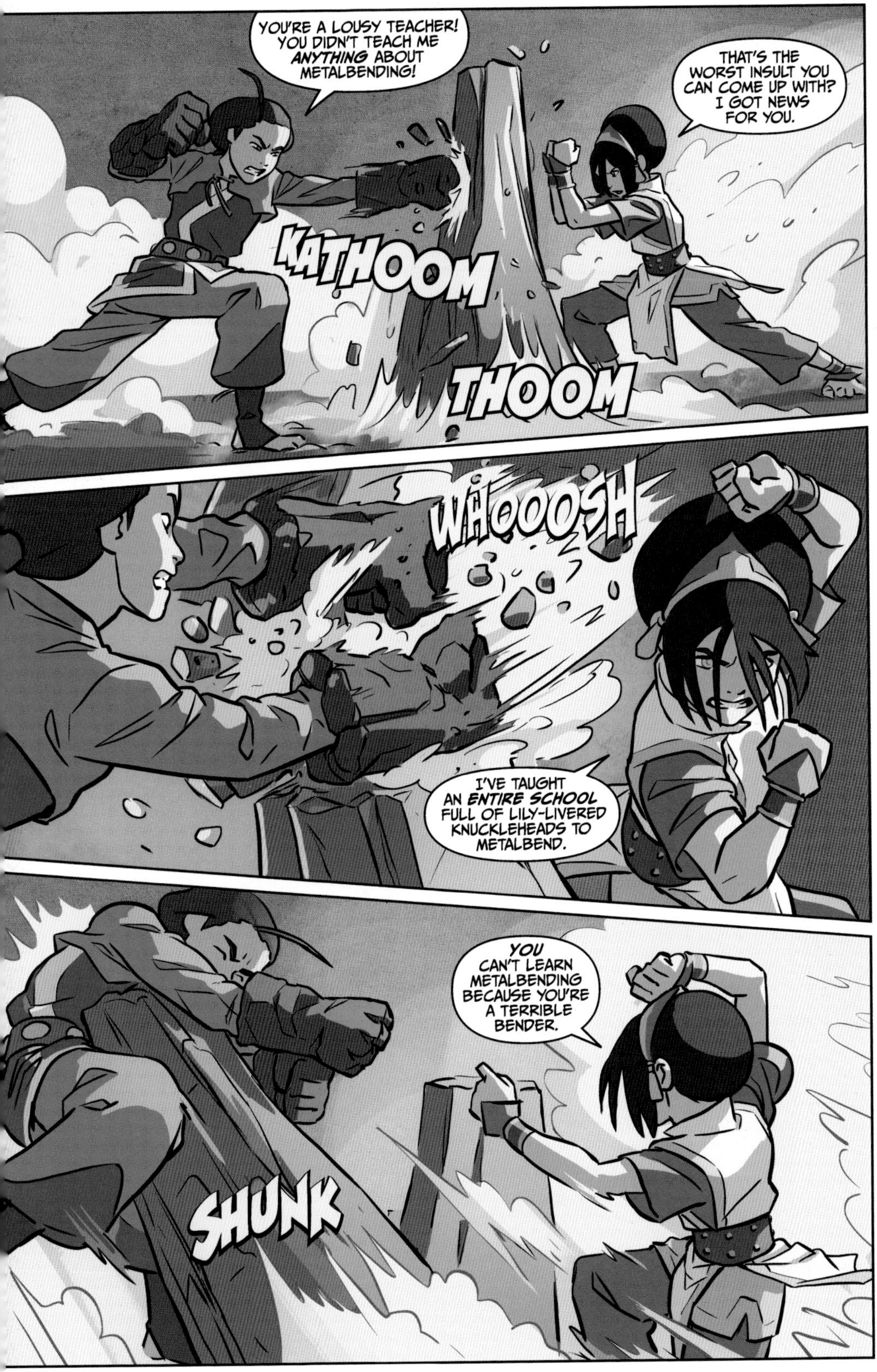
YOU'RE A LOUSY TEACHER! YOU DIDN'T TEACH ME *ANYTHING* ABOUT METALBENDING!
THAT'S THE WORST INSULT YOU CAN COME UP WITH? I GOT NEWS FOR YOU.
KATHOOM
THOOM
WHOOOSH
I'VE TAUGHT AN *ENTIRE SCHOOL* FULL OF LILY-LIVERED KNUCKLEHEADS TO METALBEND.
YOU CAN'T LEARN METALBENDING BECAUSE YOU'RE A TERRIBLE BENDER.
SHUNK

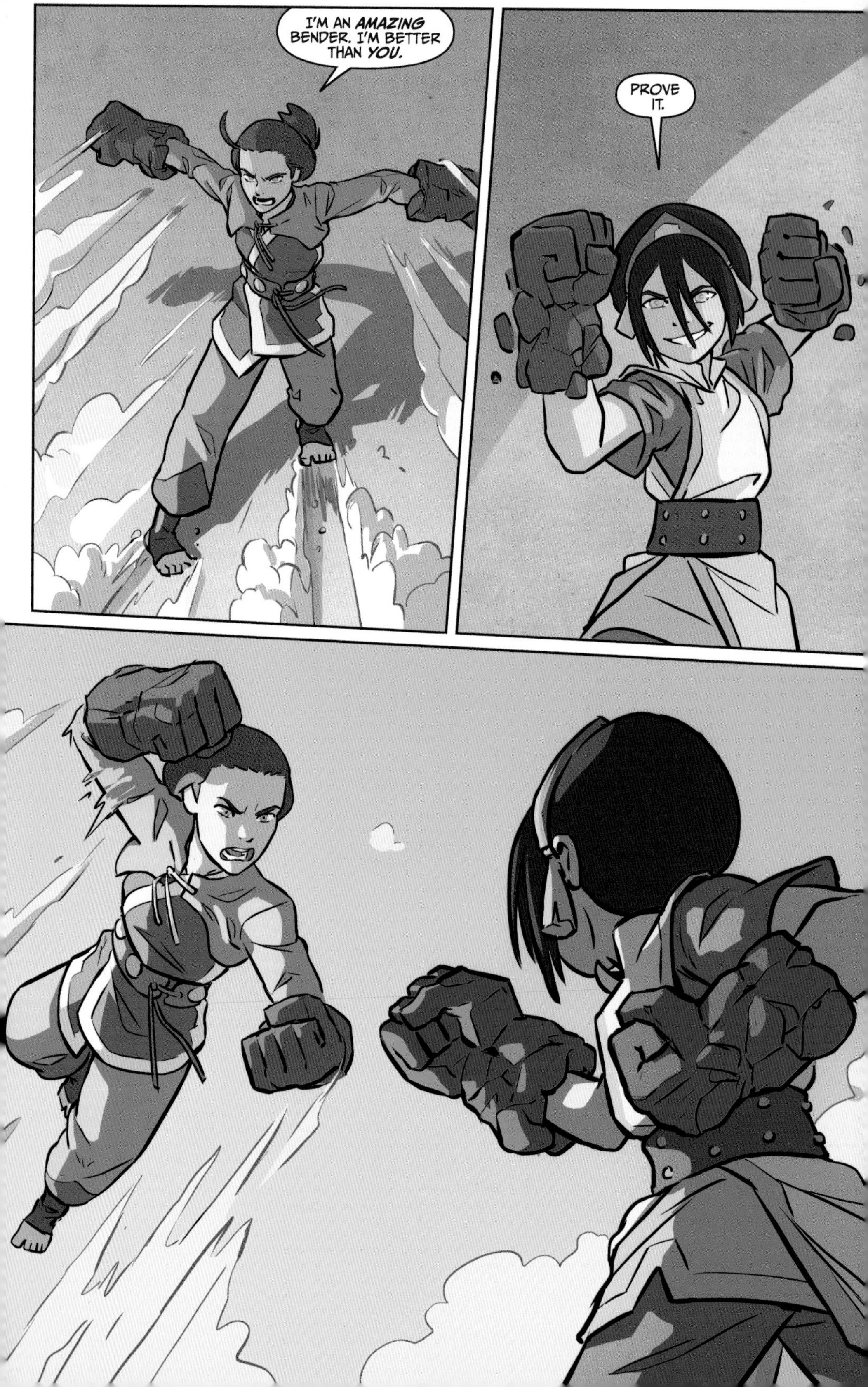
I'M AN *AMAZING* BENDER. I'M BETTER THAN *YOU.*
PROVE IT.

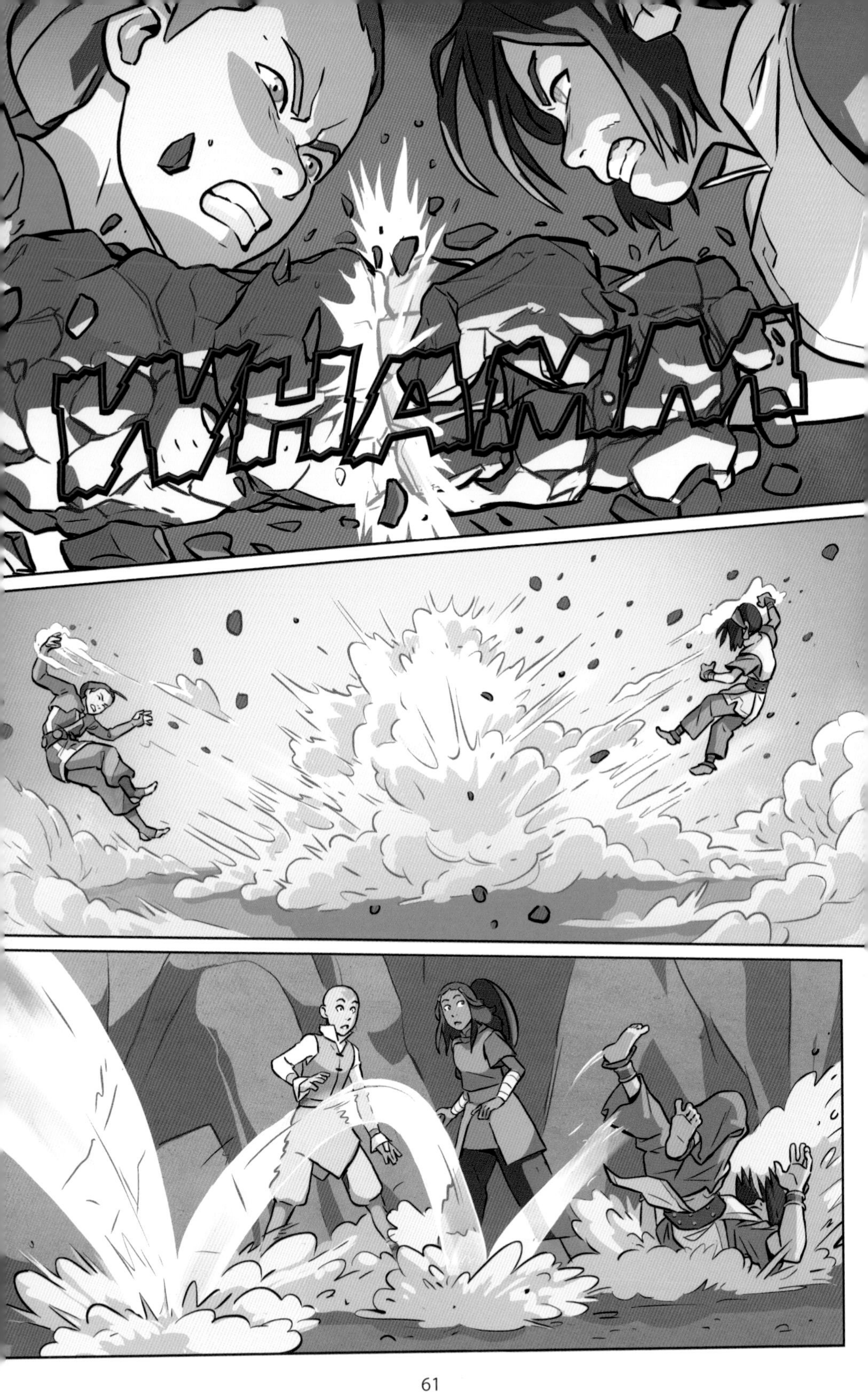
KKHAMM!

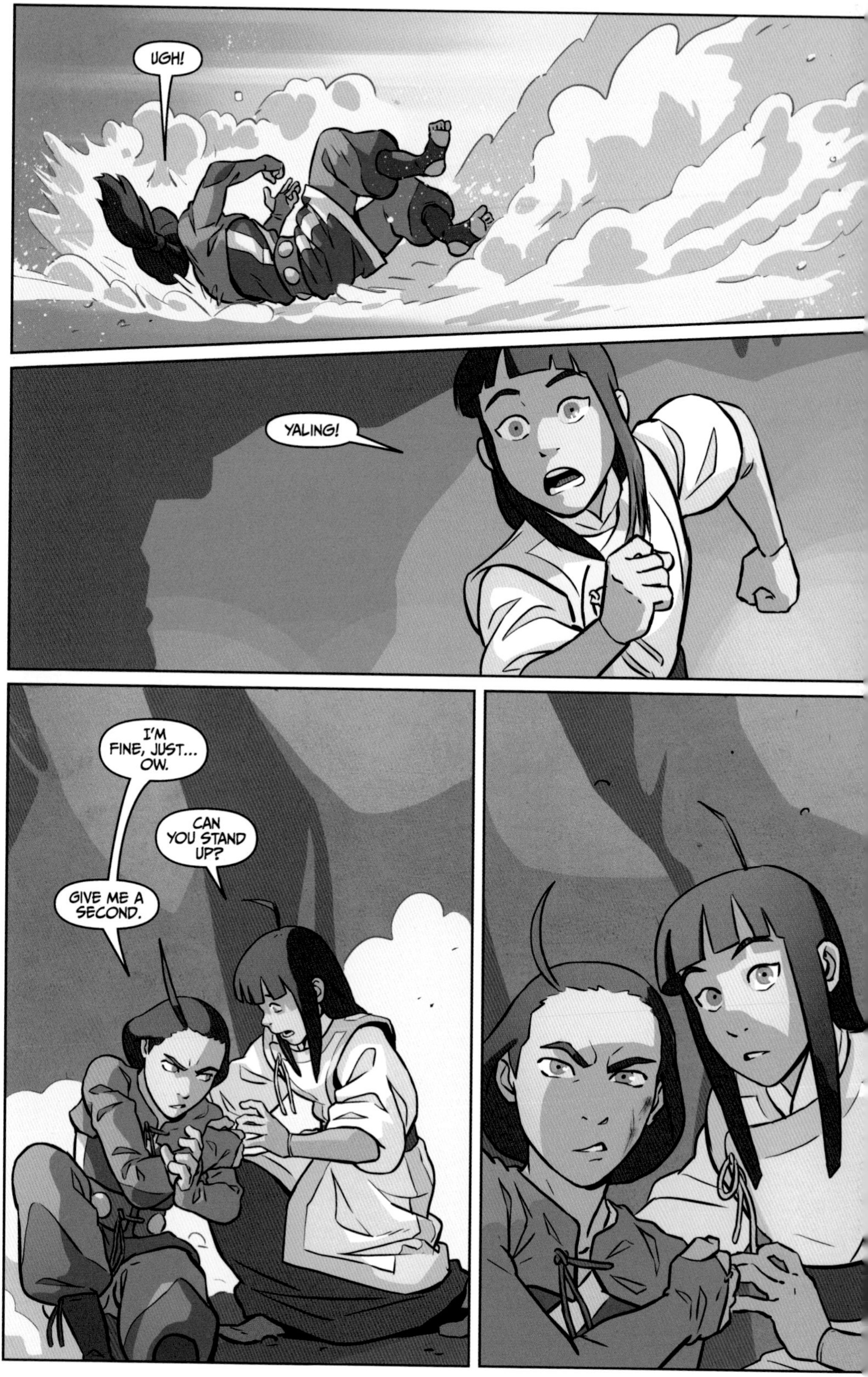
UGH!
YALING!
I'M FINE, JUST... OW.
CAN YOU STAND UP?
GIVE ME A SECOND.

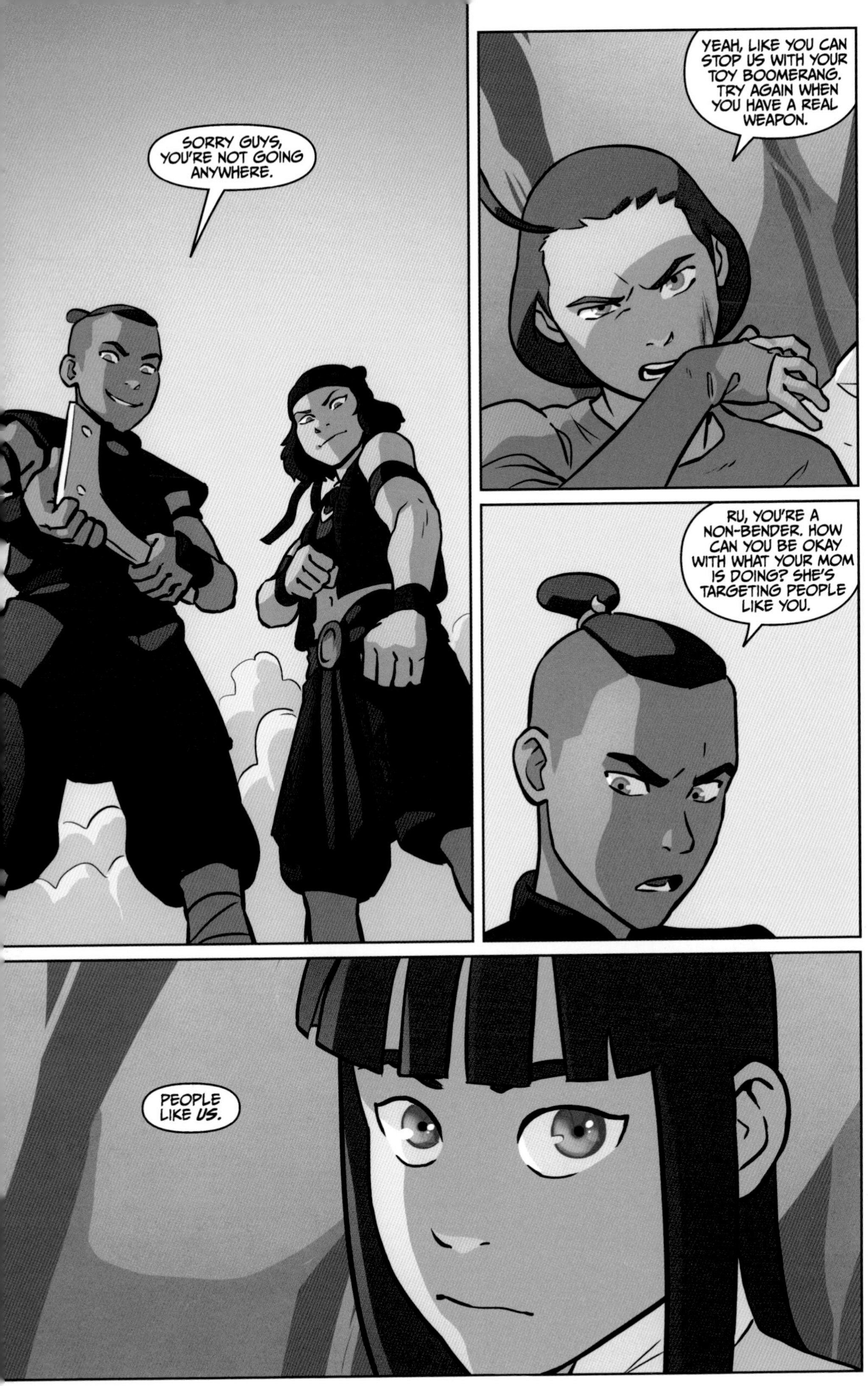
SORRY GUYS, YOU'RE NOT GOING ANYWHERE.
YEAH, LIKE YOU CAN STOP US WITH YOUR TOY BOOMERANG. TRY AGAIN WHEN YOU HAVE A REAL WEAPON.
RU, YOU'RE A NON-BENDER. HOW CAN YOU BE OKAY WITH WHAT YOUR MOM IS DOING? SHE'S TARGETING PEOPLE LIKE YOU.
PEOPLE LIKE *US*.

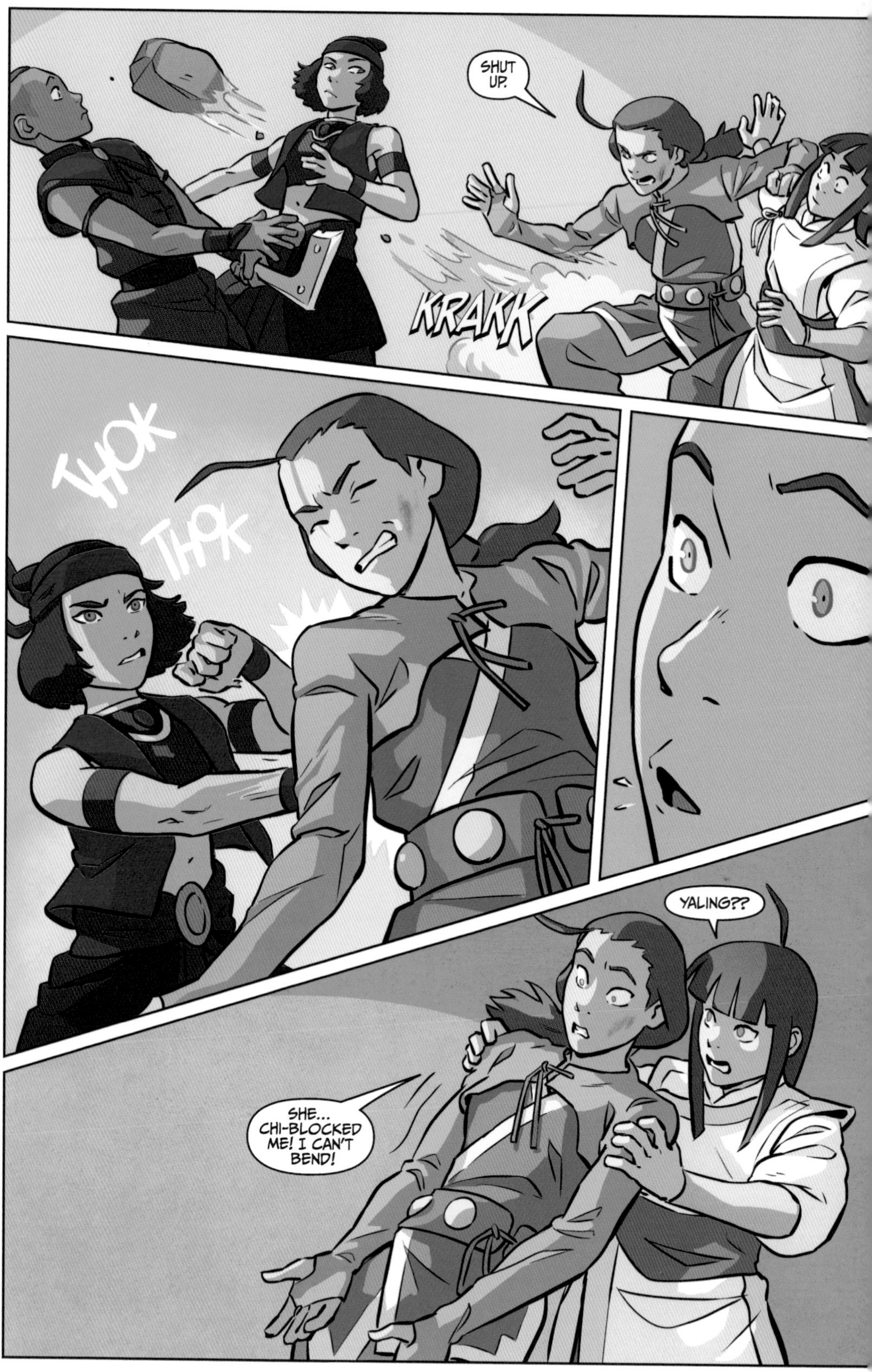
SHUT UP.
KRAKK
THOK
THOK
YALING??
SHE... CHI-BLOCKED ME! I CAN'T BEND!

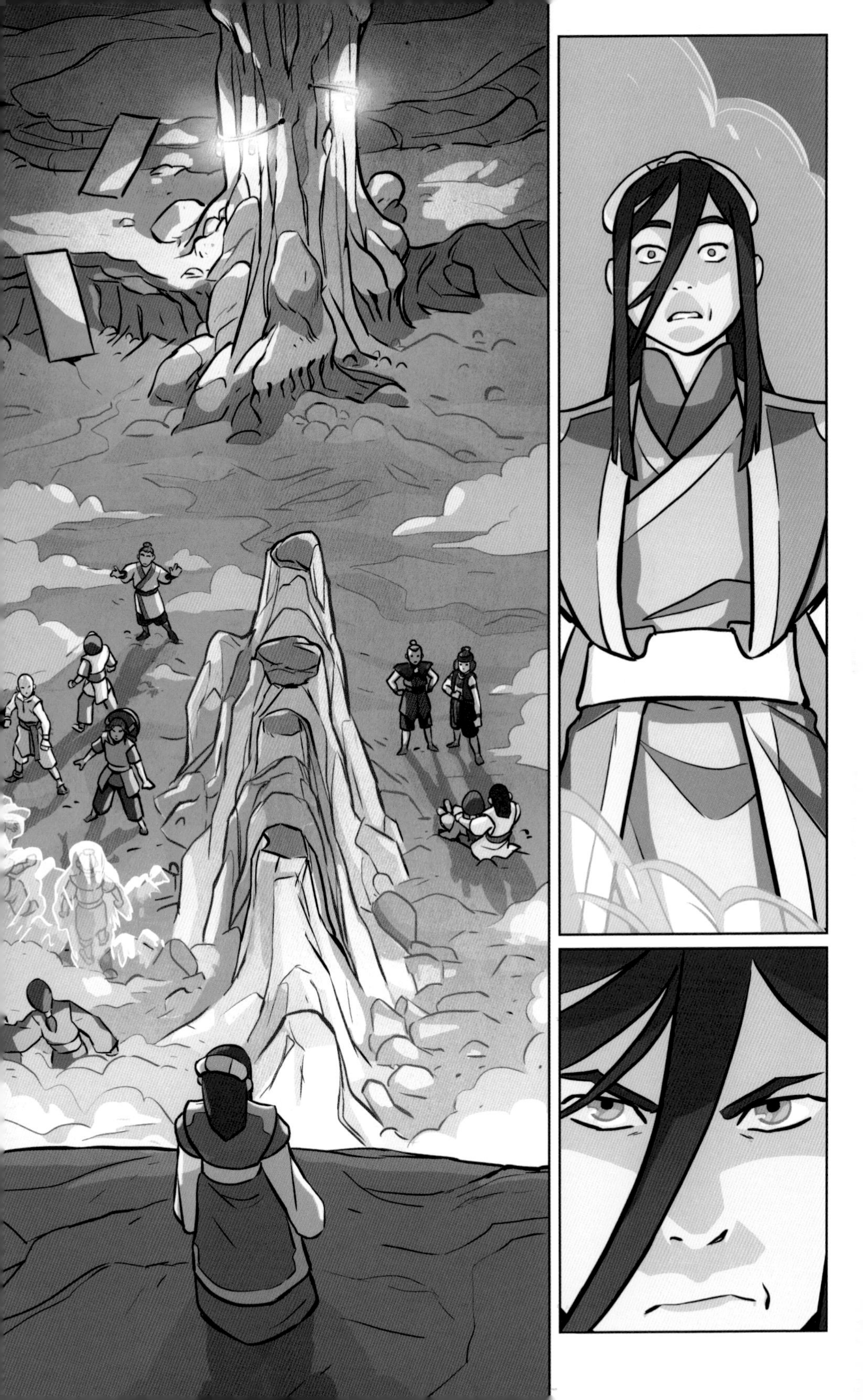

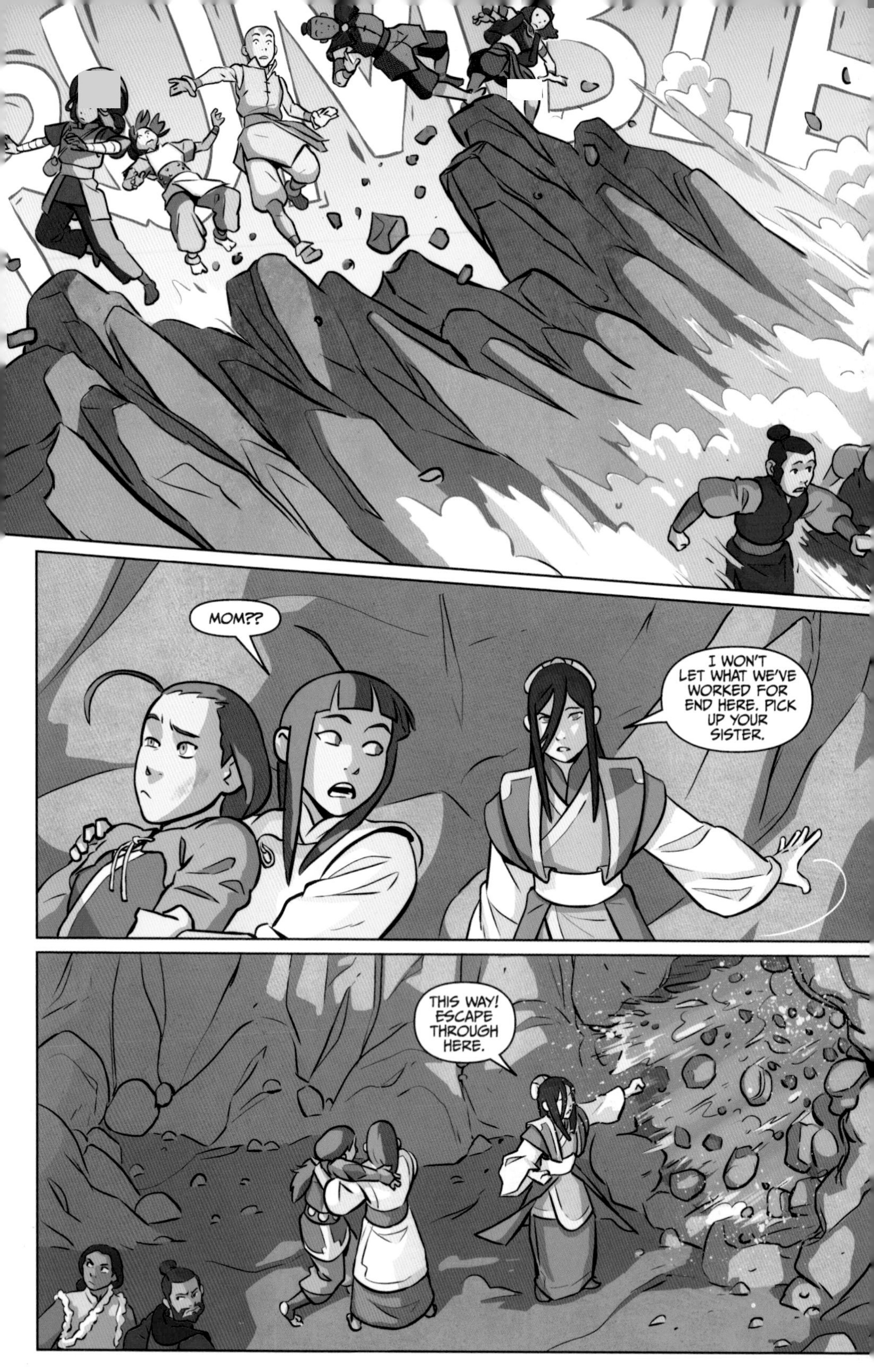
MOM??
I WON'T LET WHAT WE'VE WORKED FOR END HERE. PICK UP YOUR SISTER.
THIS WAY! ESCAPE THROUGH HERE.

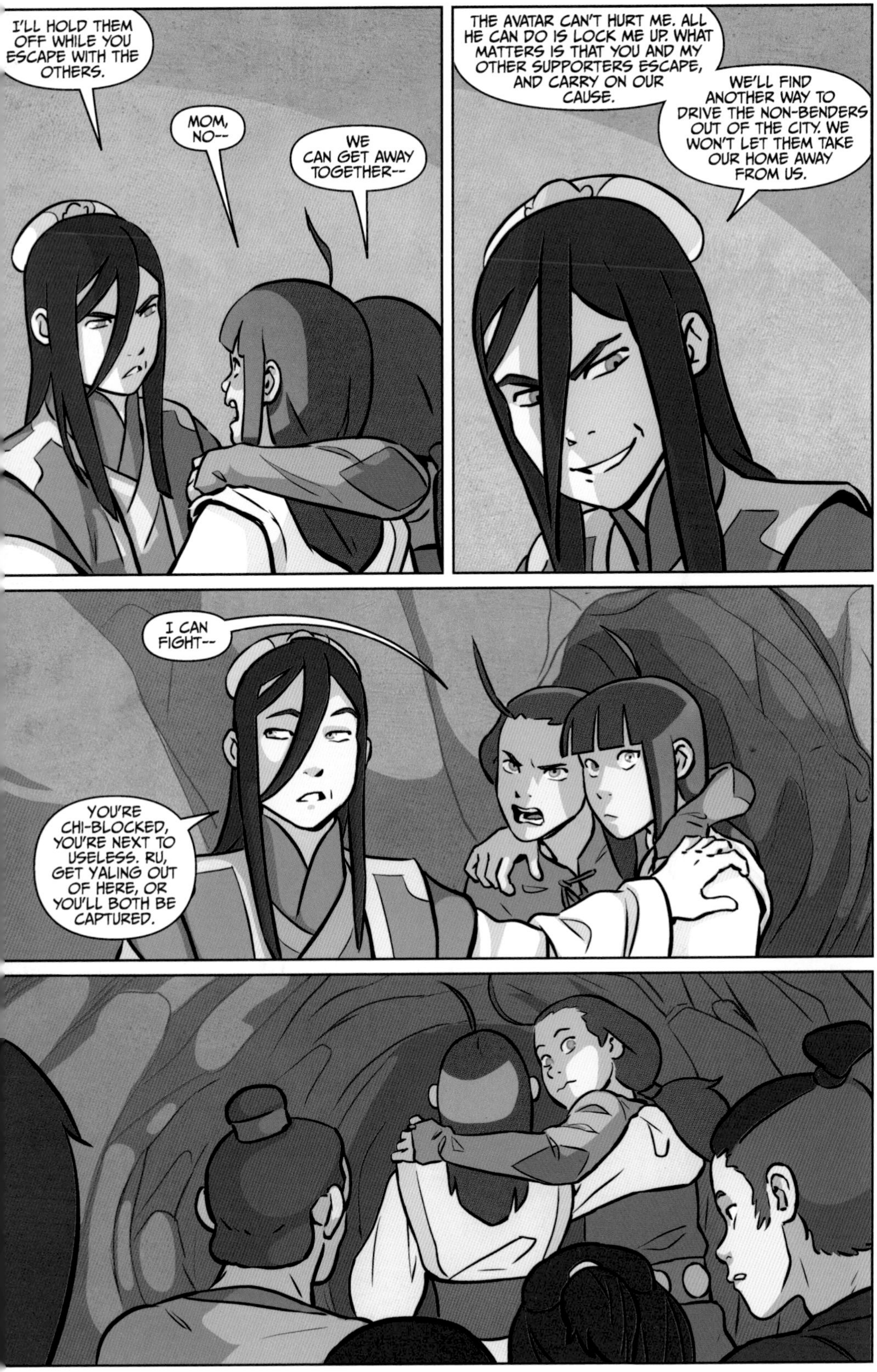
I'LL HOLD THEM OFF WHILE YOU ESCAPE WITH THE OTHERS.
MOM, NO--
WE CAN GET AWAY TOGETHER--
THE AVATAR CAN'T HURT ME. ALL HE CAN DO IS LOCK ME UP. WHAT MATTERS IS THAT YOU AND MY OTHER SUPPORTERS ESCAPE, AND CARRY ON OUR CAUSE.
WE'LL FIND ANOTHER WAY TO DRIVE THE NON-BENDERS OUT OF THE CITY. WE WON'T LET THEM TAKE OUR HOME AWAY FROM US.
I CAN FIGHT--
YOU'RE CHI-BLOCKED, YOU'RE NEXT TO USELESS. RU, GET YALING OUT OF HERE, OR YOU'LL BOTH BE CAPTURED.

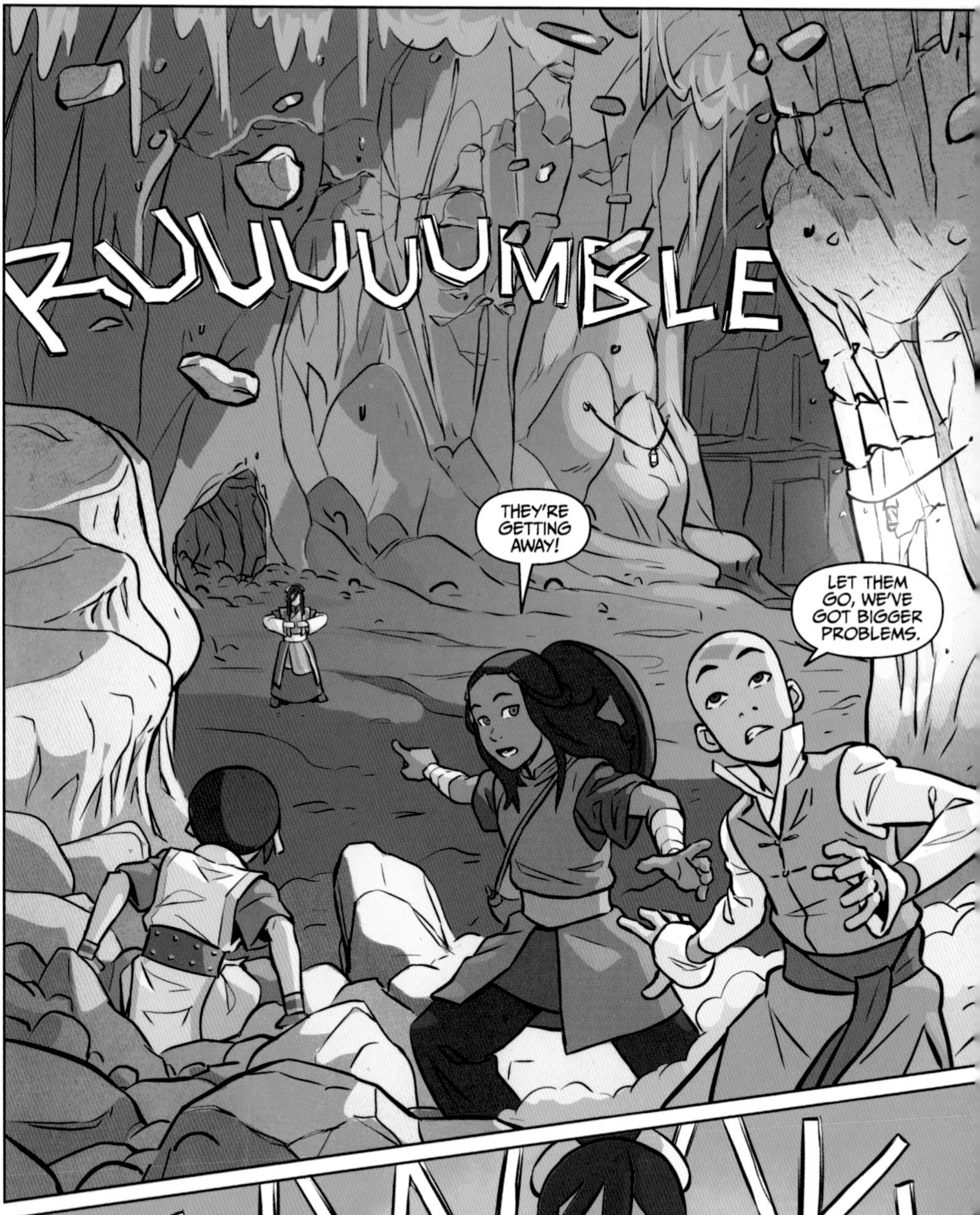
RUUUUUMBLE
THEY'RE GETTING AWAY!
LET THEM GO, WE'VE GOT BIGGER PROBLEMS.

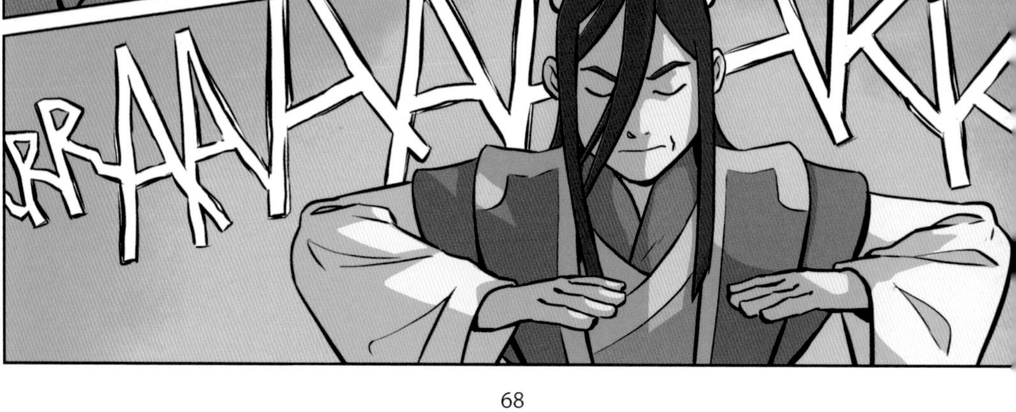
RRAAAAKK

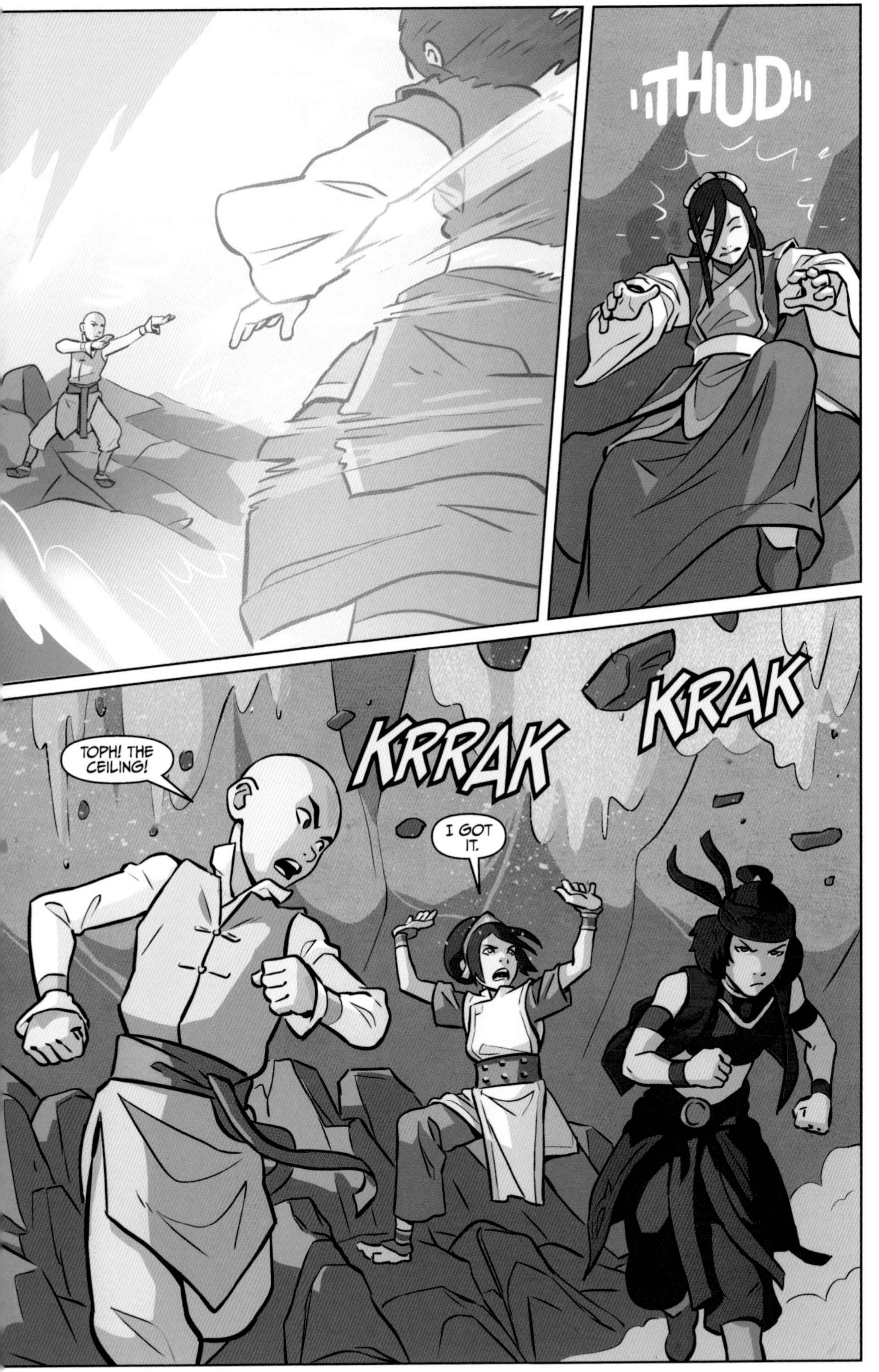
THUD
TOPH! THE CEILING!
KRRAK
KRAK
I GOT IT.

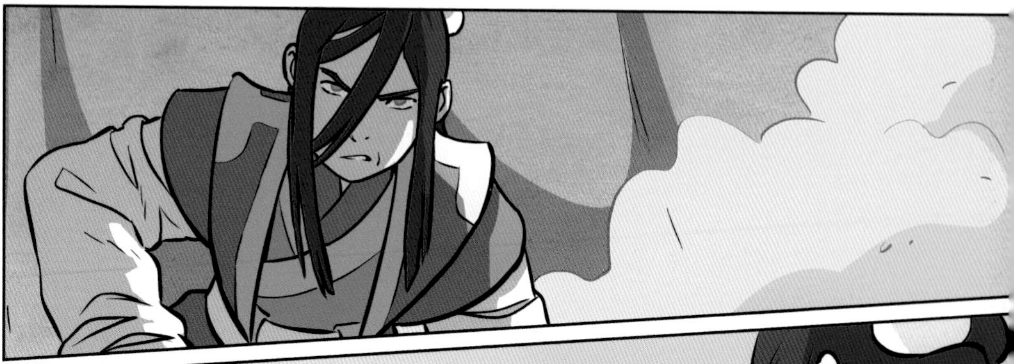

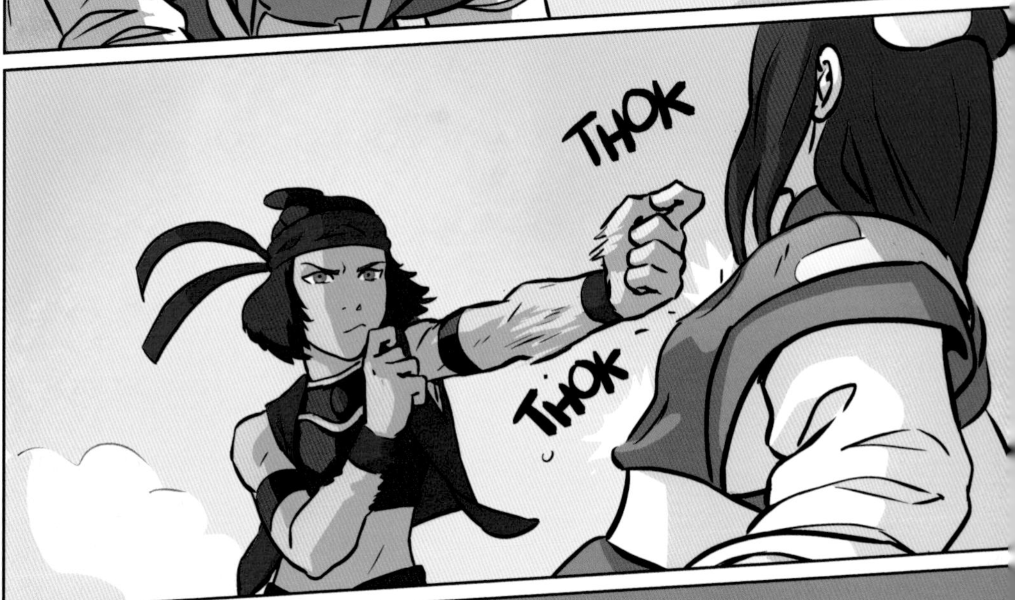
THOK
THOK

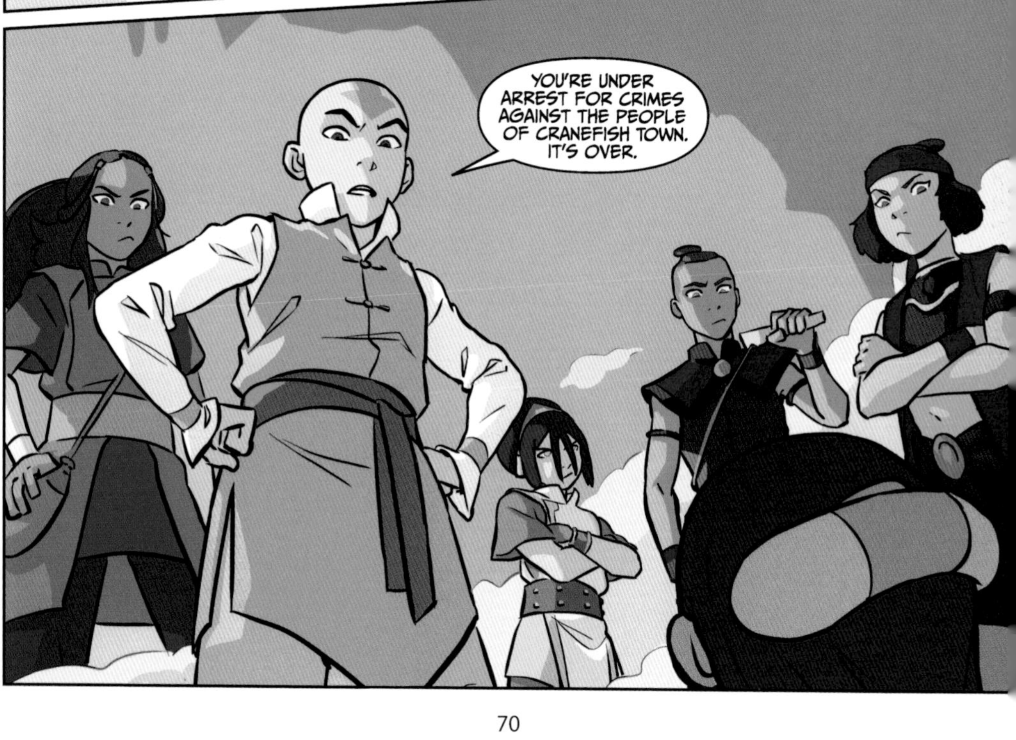
YOU'RE UNDER ARREST FOR CRIMES AGAINST THE PEOPLE OF CRANEFISH TOWN. IT'S OVER.

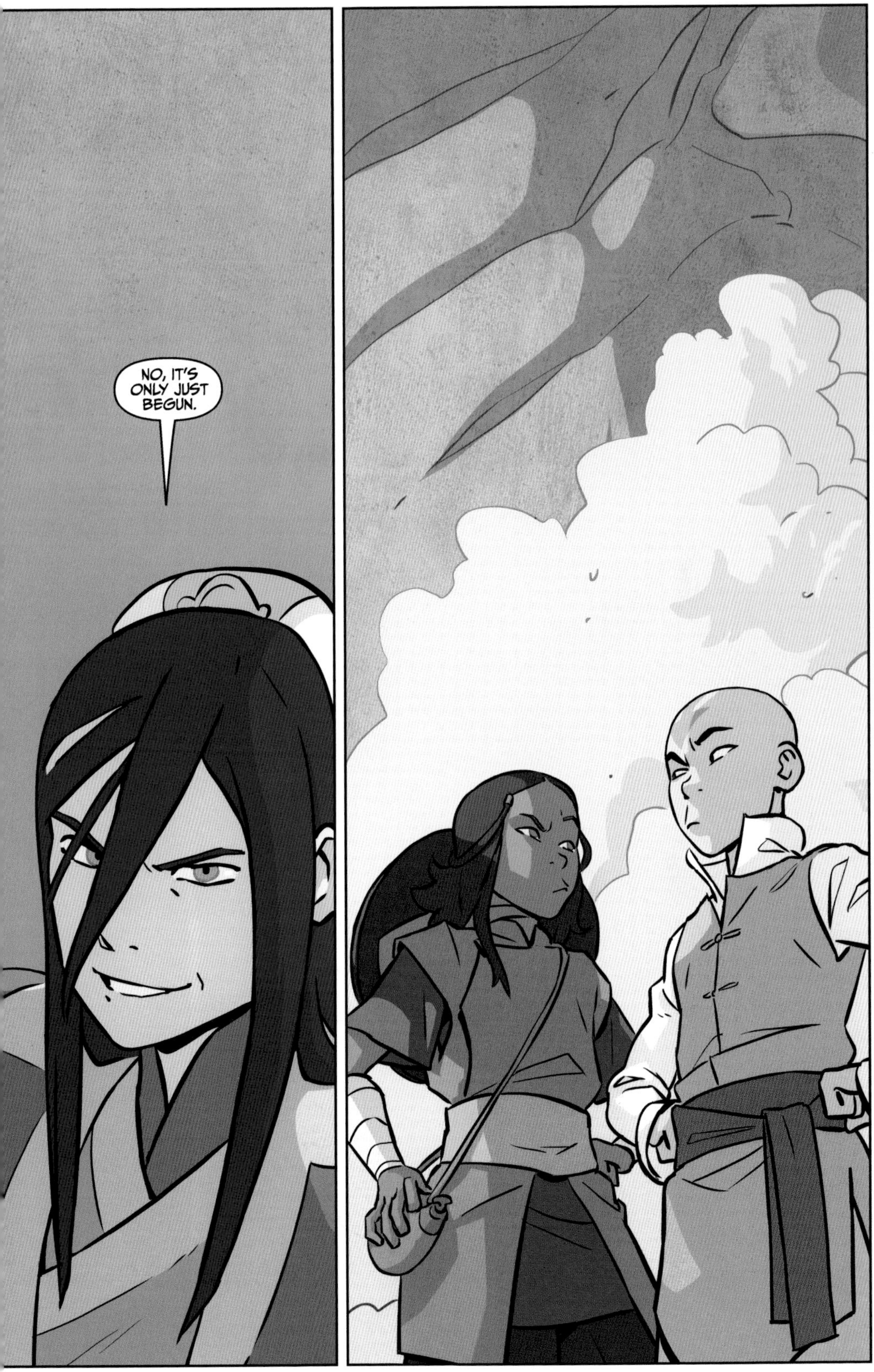
NO, IT'S ONLY JUST BEGUN.

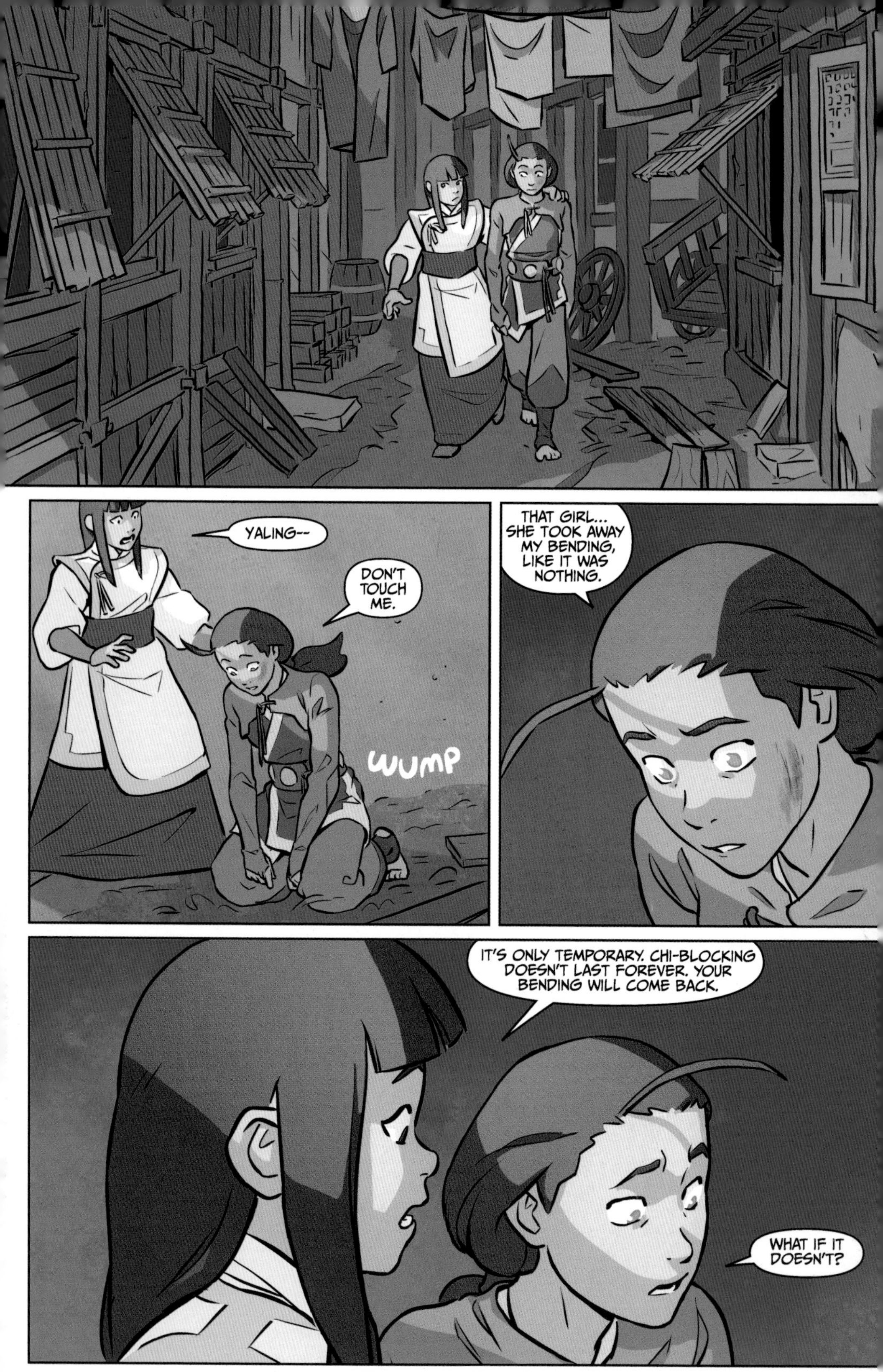
YALING--
DON'T TOUCH ME.
WUMP
THAT GIRL... SHE TOOK AWAY MY BENDING, LIKE IT WAS NOTHING.
IT'S ONLY TEMPORARY. CHI-BLOCKING DOESN'T LAST FOREVER. YOUR BENDING WILL COME BACK.
WHAT IF IT DOESN'T?

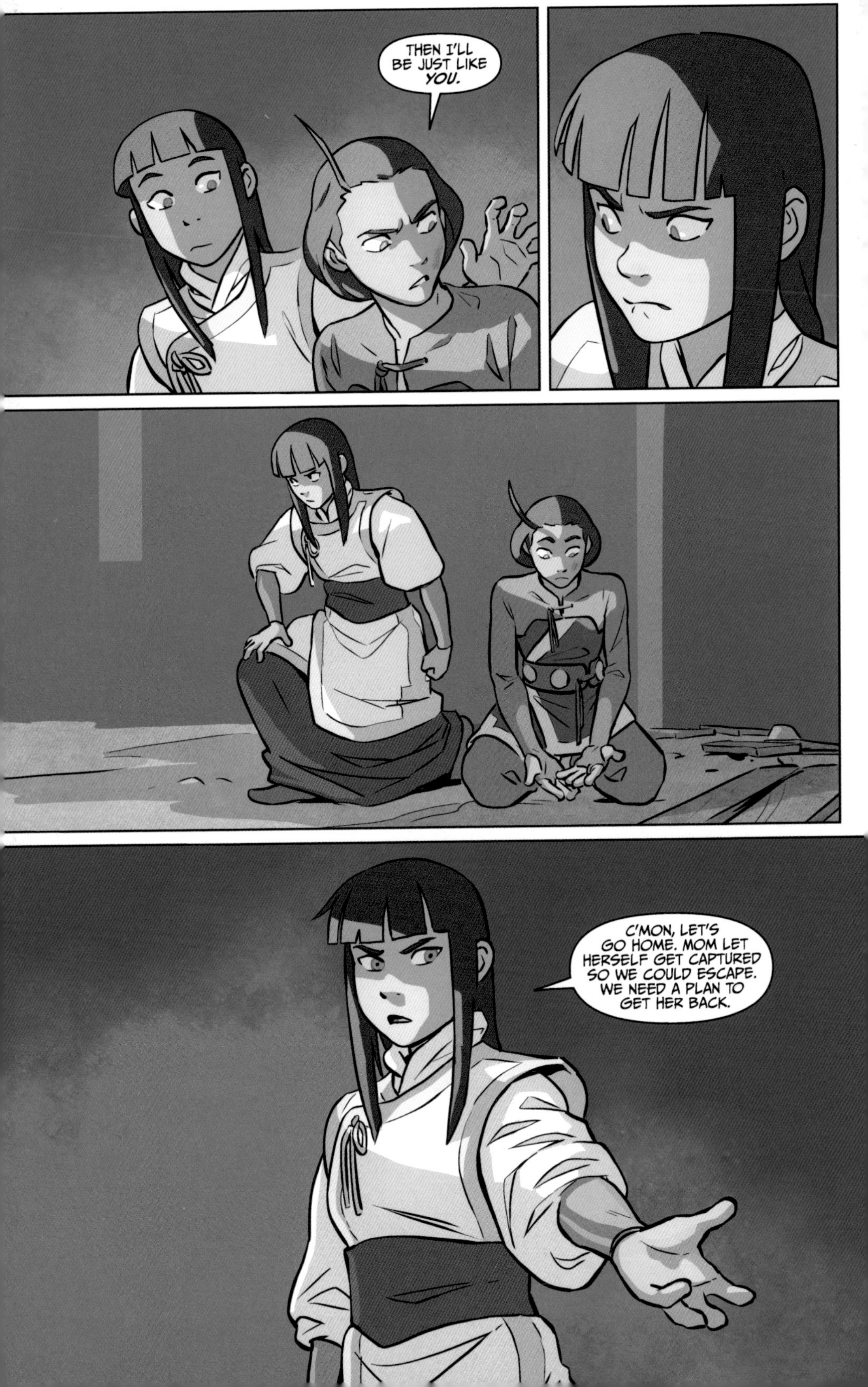
THEN I'LL BE JUST LIKE YOU.
C'MON, LET'S GO HOME. MOM LET HERSELF GET CAPTURED SO WE COULD ESCAPE. WE NEED A PLAN TO GET HER BACK.

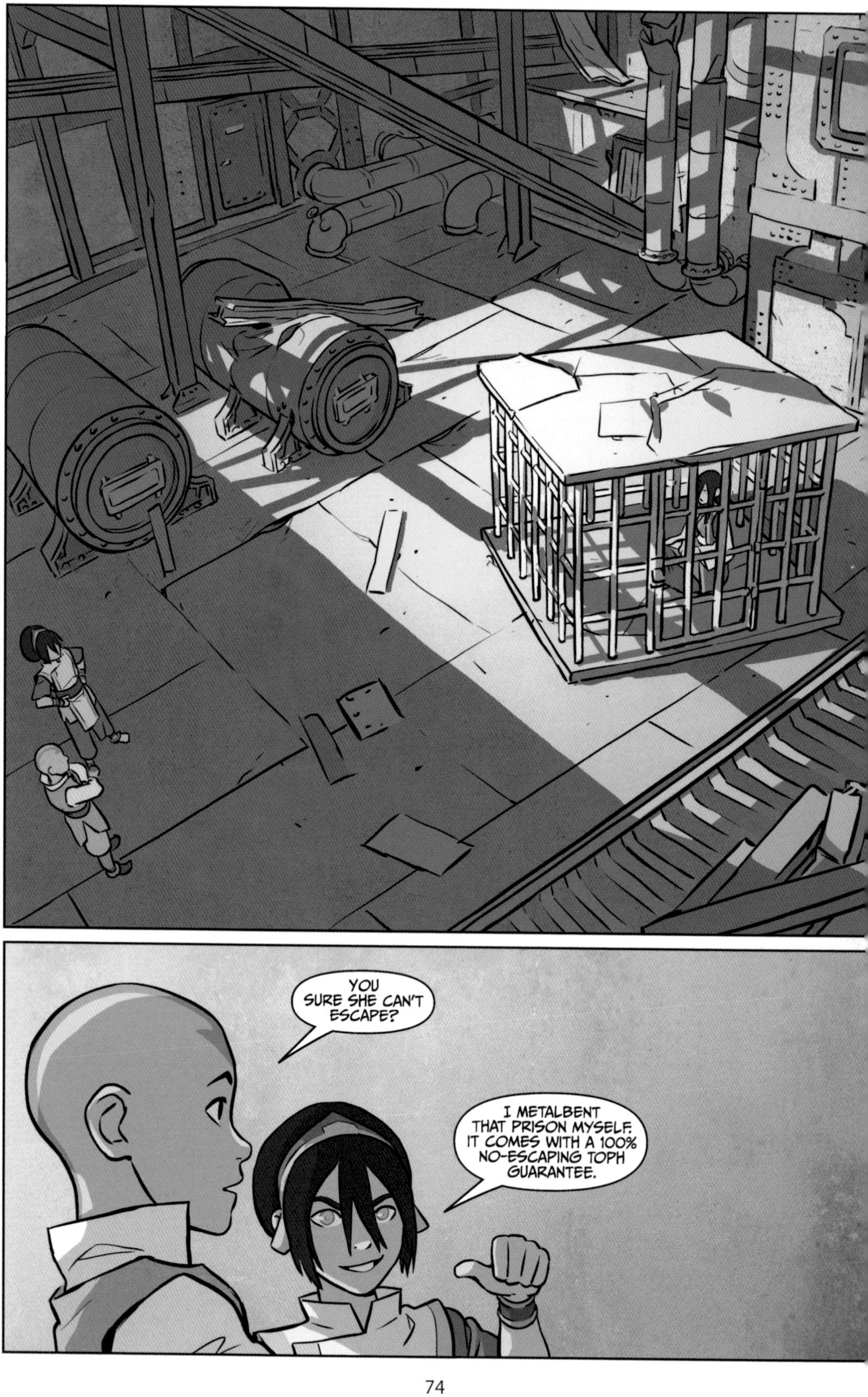
YOU SURE SHE CAN'T ESCAPE?
I METALBENT THAT PRISON MYSELF. IT COMES WITH A 100% NO-ESCAPING TOPH GUARANTEE.

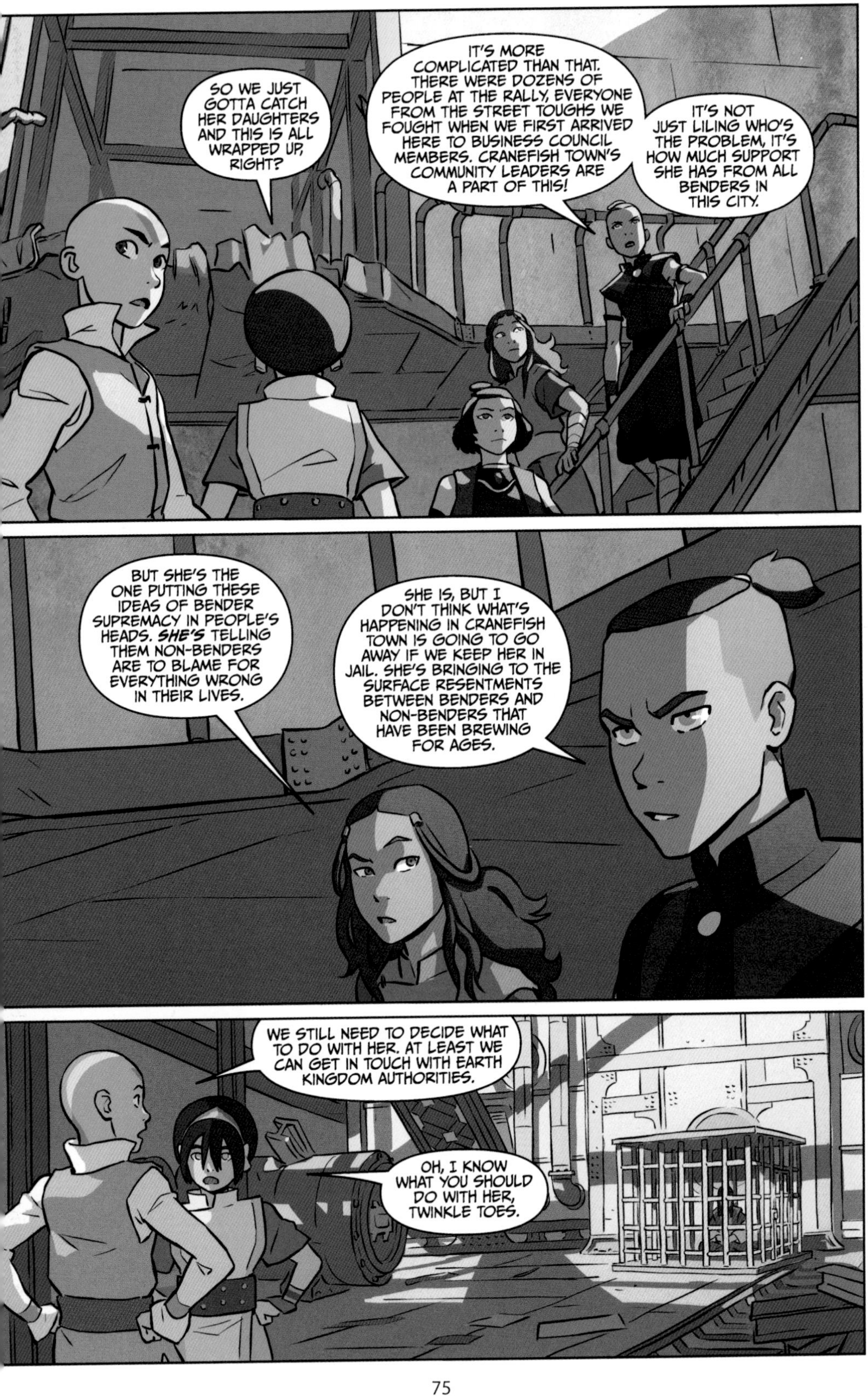
SO WE JUST GOTTA CATCH HER DAUGHTERS AND THIS IS ALL WRAPPED UP, RIGHT?
IT'S MORE COMPLICATED THAN THAT. THERE WERE DOZENS OF PEOPLE AT THE RALLY, EVERYONE FROM THE STREET TOUGHS WE FOUGHT WHEN WE FIRST ARRIVED HERE TO BUSINESS COUNCIL MEMBERS. CRANEFISH TOWN'S COMMUNITY LEADERS ARE A PART OF THIS!
IT'S NOT JUST LILING WHO'S THE PROBLEM, IT'S HOW MUCH SUPPORT SHE HAS FROM ALL BENDERS IN THIS CITY.
BUT SHE'S THE ONE PUTTING THESE IDEAS OF BENDER SUPREMACY IN PEOPLE'S HEADS. ***SHE'S*** TELLING THEM NON-BENDERS ARE TO BLAME FOR EVERYTHING WRONG IN THEIR LIVES.
SHE IS, BUT I DON'T THINK WHAT'S HAPPENING IN CRANEFISH TOWN IS GOING TO GO AWAY IF WE KEEP HER IN JAIL. SHE'S BRINGING TO THE SURFACE RESENTMENTS BETWEEN BENDERS AND NON-BENDERS THAT HAVE BEEN BREWING FOR AGES.
WE STILL NEED TO DECIDE WHAT TO DO WITH HER. AT LEAST WE CAN GET IN TOUCH WITH EARTH KINGDOM AUTHORITIES.
OH, I KNOW WHAT YOU SHOULD DO WITH HER, TWINKLE TOES.

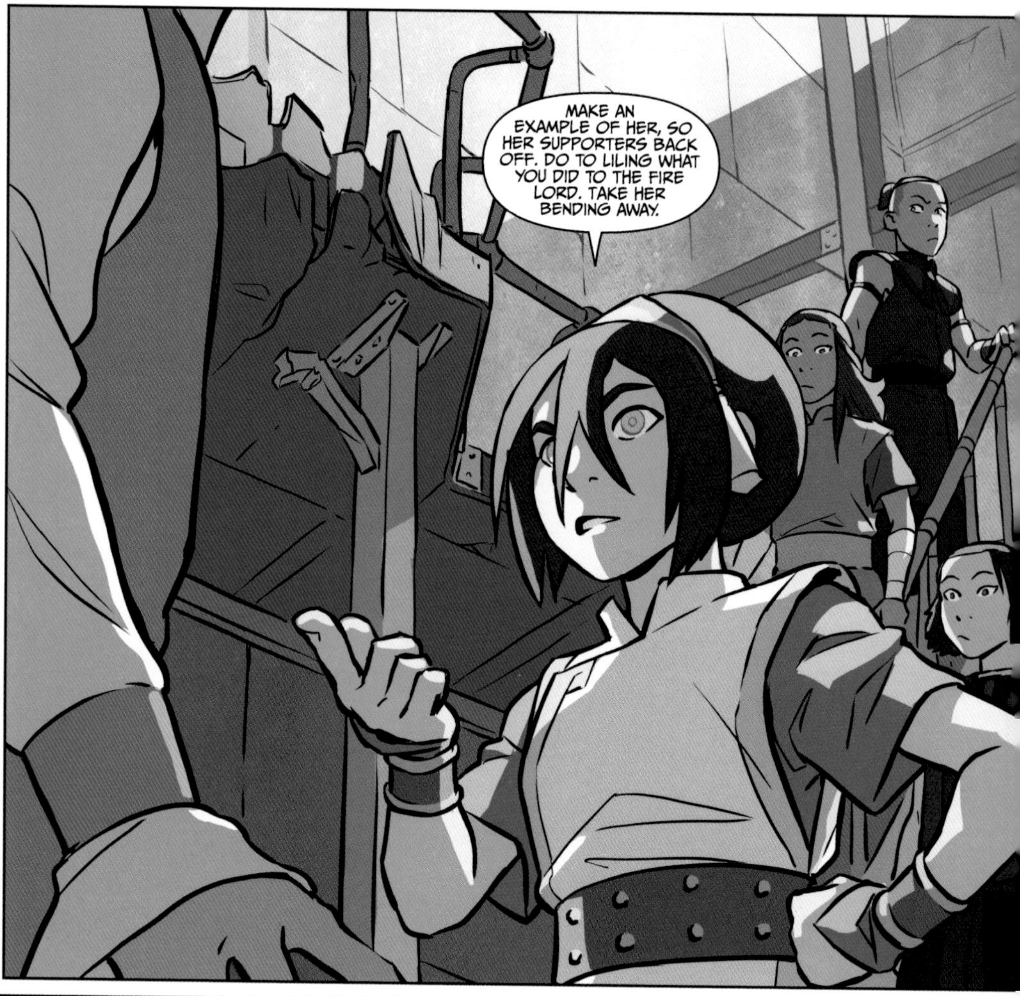
MAKE AN EXAMPLE OF HER, SO HER SUPPORTERS BACK OFF. DO TO LILING WHAT YOU DID TO THE FIRE LORD. TAKE HER BENDING AWAY.

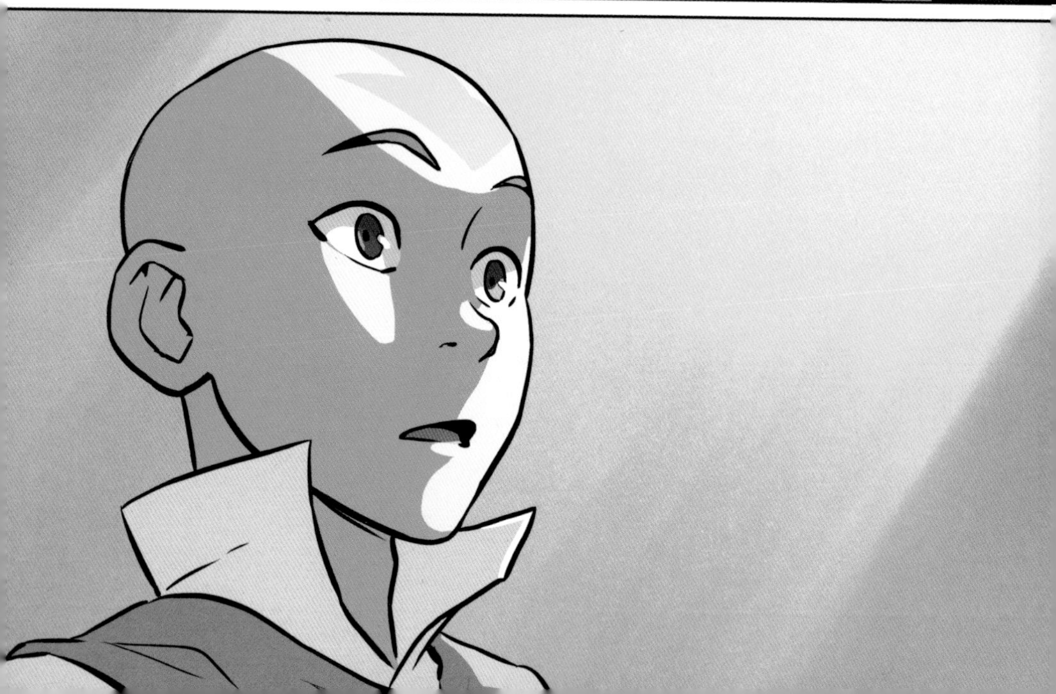

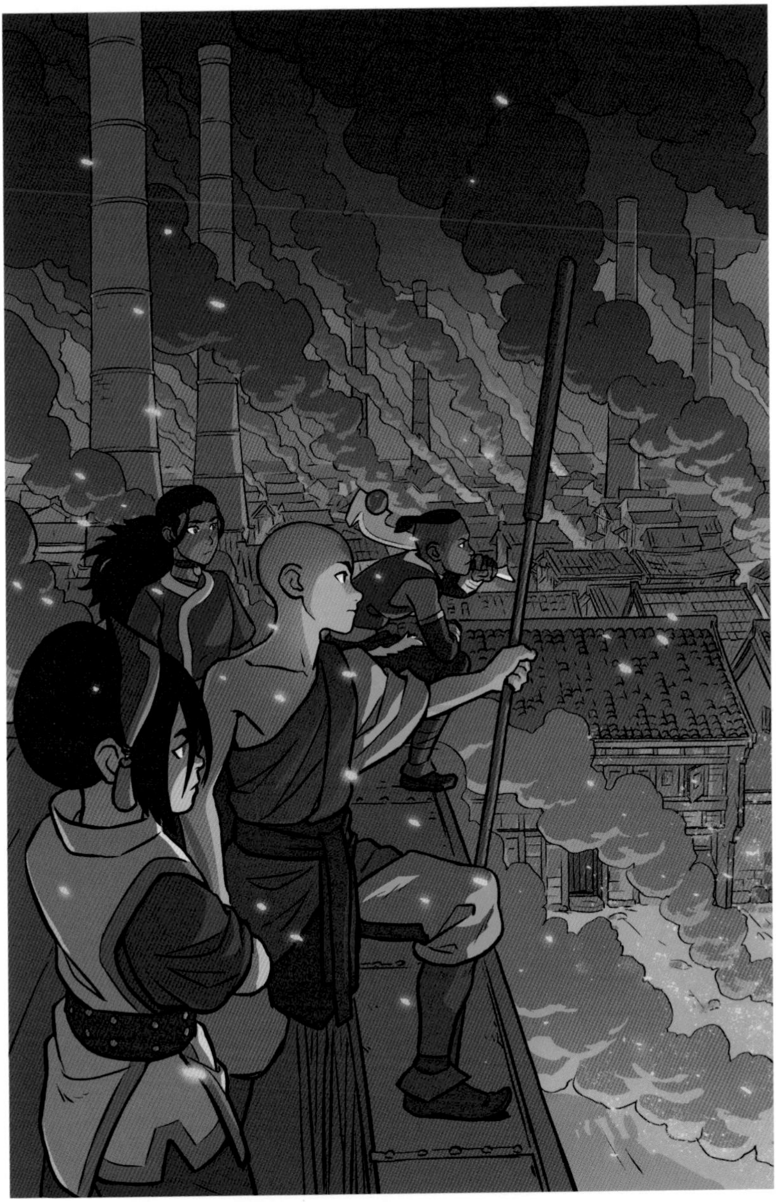

COMING IN SEPTEMBER 2019!

What will it take to uncover the source of prejudice?

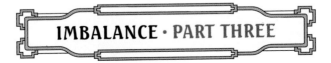

IMBALANCE • PART THREE

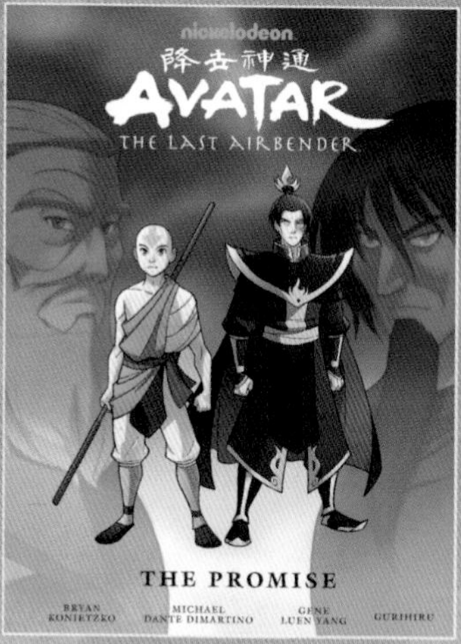
nickelodeon
AVATAR
THE LAST AIRBENDER
THE PROMISE
BRYAN KONIETZKO
MICHAEL DANTE DIMARTINO
GENE LUEN YANG
GURIHIRU

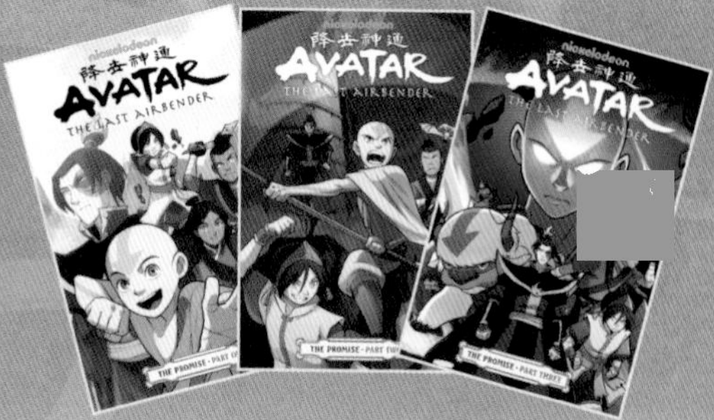
AVATAR
THE LAST AIRBENDER

Avatar: The Last Airbender—The Promise Library Edition
978-1-61655-074-5 $39.99

Avatar: The Last Airbender—The Promise Part 1
978-1-59582-811-8 $10.99

Avatar: The Last Airbender—The Promise Part 2
978-1-59582-875-0 $10.99

Avatar: The Last Airbender—The Promise Part 3
978-1-59582-941-2 $10.99

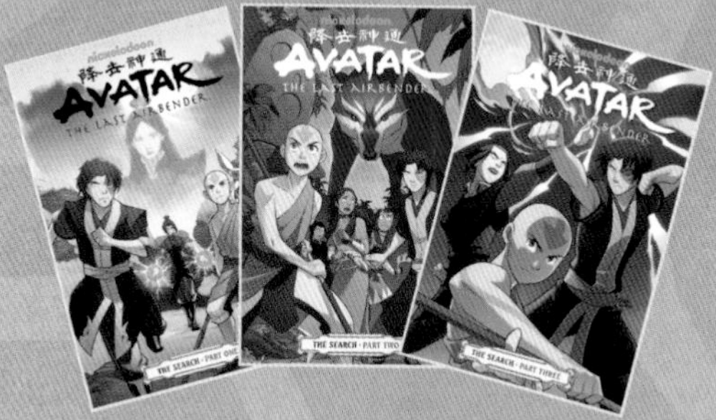
AVATAR
THE LAST AIRBENDER

Avatar: The Last Airbender—The Search Library Edition
978-1-61655-226-8 $39.99

Avatar: The Last Airbender—The Search Part 1
978-1-61655-054-7 $10.99

Avatar: The Last Airbender—The Search Part 2
978-1-61655-190-2 $10.99

Avatar: The Last Airbender—The Search Part 3
978-1-61655-184-1 $10.99

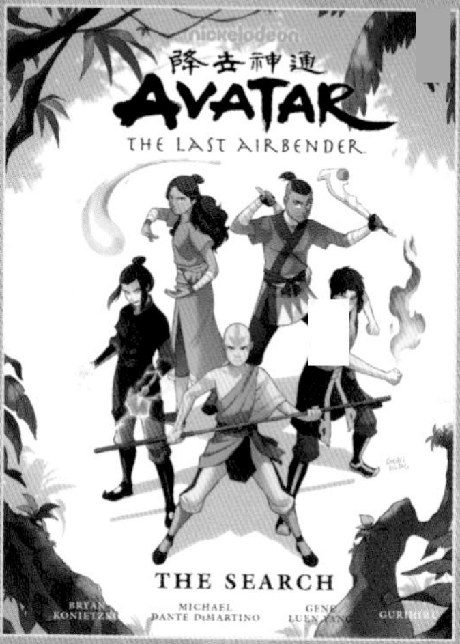
nickelodeon
AVATAR
THE LAST AIRBENDER
THE SEARCH
BRYAN KONIETZKO
MICHAEL DANTE DiMARTINO
GENE LUEN YANG
GURIHIRU

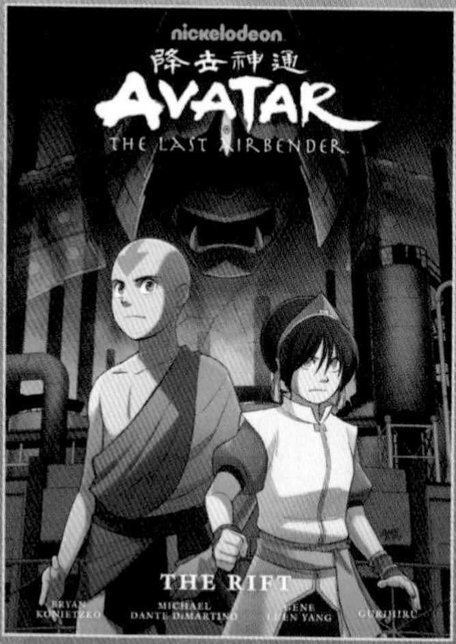
nickelodeon
AVATAR
THE LAST AIRBENDER
THE RIFT
BRYAN KONIETZKO
MICHAEL DANTE DiMARTINO
GENE LUEN YANG
GURIHIRU

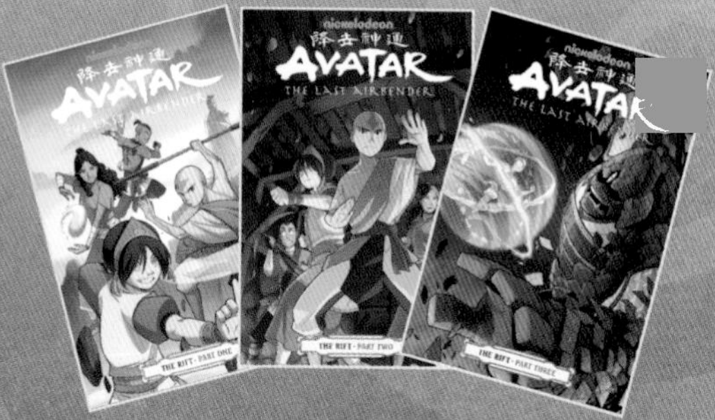
AVATAR
THE LAST AIRBENDER

Avatar: The Last Airbender—The Rift Library Edition
978-1-61655-550-4 $39.99

Avatar: The Last Airbender—The Rift Part 1
978-1-61655-295-4 $10.99

Avatar: The Last Airbender—The Rift Part 2
978-1-61655-296-1 $10.99

Avatar: The Last Airbender—The Rift Part 3
978-1-61655-297-8 $10.99

nickelodeon
降去神通
AVATAR
THE LAST AIRBENDER
SMOKE AND SHADOW · PART THREE

nickelodeon
降去神通
AVATAR
THE LAST AIRBENDER
SMOKE AND SHADOW

Avatar: The Last Airbender—Smoke and Shadow Library Edition
978-1-50670-013-7 $39.99

Avatar: The Last Airbender—Smoke and Shadow Part 1
978-1-61655-761-4 $10.99

Avatar: The Last Airbender—Smoke and Shadow Part 2
978-1-61655-790-4 $10.99

Avatar: The Last Airbender—Smoke and Shadow Part 3
978-1-61655-838-3 $10.99

nickelodeon
降去神通
AVATAR
THE LAST AIRBENDER
NORTH AND SOUTH
BRYAN KONIETZKO
MICHAEL DANTE DiMARTINO
GENE LUEN YANG
GURIHIRU

NORTH AND SOUTH · PART THREE

Avatar: The Last Airbender—North and South Part 1
978-1-50670-022-9 $10.99

Avatar: The Last Airbender—North and South Part 2
978-1-50670-129-5 $10.99

Avatar: The Last Airbender—North and South Part 3
978-1-50670-130-1 $10.99

Avatar: The Last Airbender—North And South Library Edition
978-1-50670-195-0 $39.99

nickelodeon
降去神通
AVATAR
THE LAST AIRBENDER
IMBALANCE · PART ONE

Avatar: The Last Airbender—The Art of the Animated Series
978-1-59582-504-9 $34.99

Avatar: The Last Airbender—The Lost Adventures
978-1-59582-748-7 $14.99

Avatar: The Last Airbender—Imbalance Part 1
978-1-50670-489-0 $10.99

降去神通
AVATAR
THE LAST AIRBENDER

BE PART OF THE INCREDIBLE JOURNEY!

Check out the best-selling graphic novels by acclaimed writer Gene Luen Yang.

AVAILABLE AT YOUR LOCAL COMICS SHOP OR BOOKSTORE! To find a comics shop in your area, visit comicshoplocator.com. For more information or to order direct visit DarkHorswe.com or call 1-800-862-0052

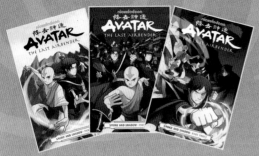

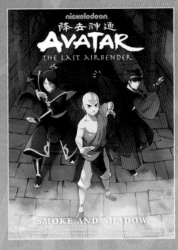

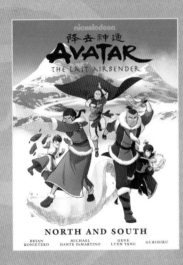

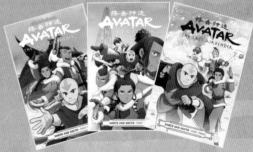

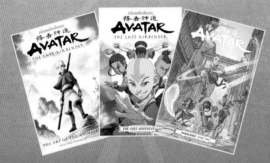

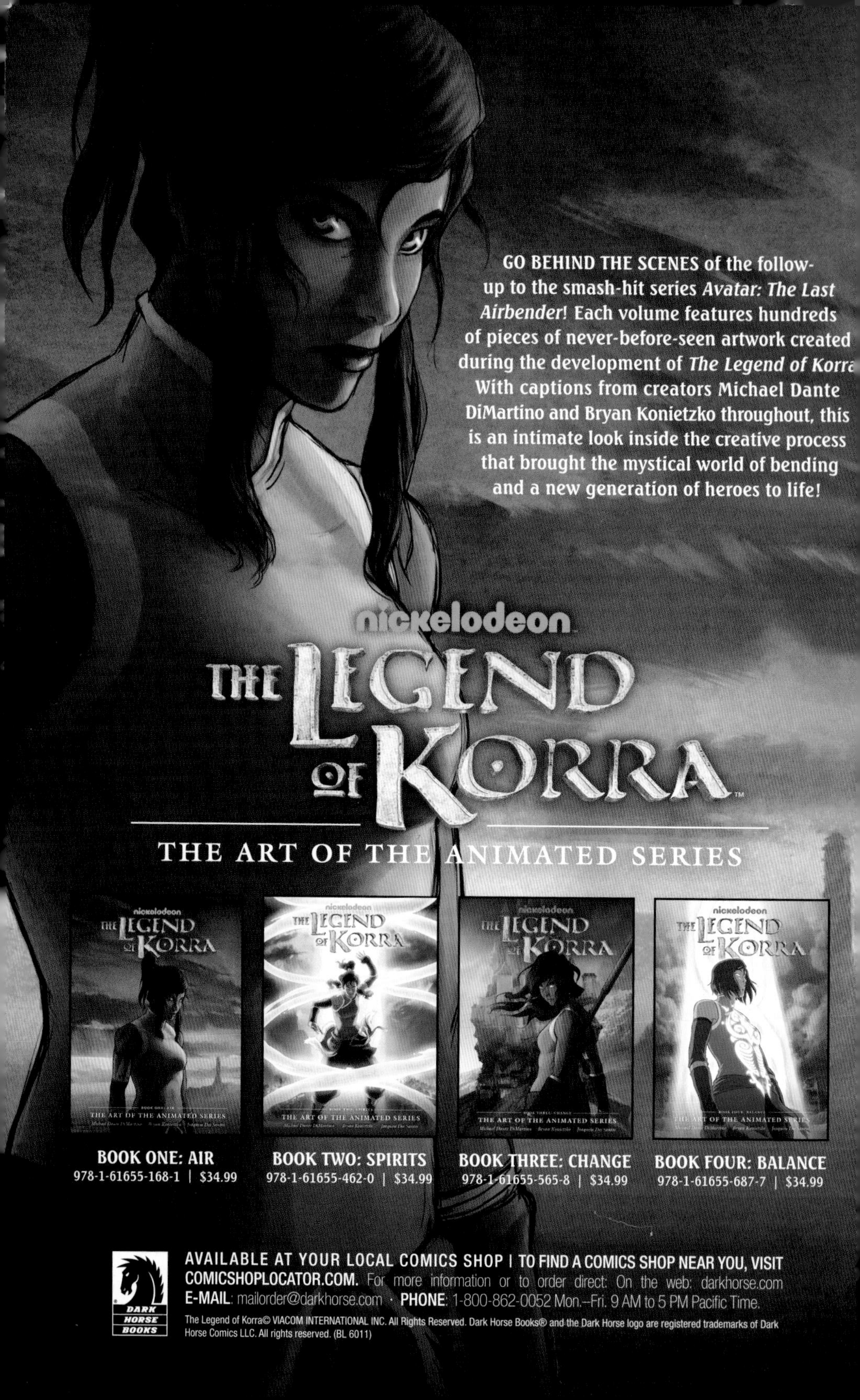
GO BEHIND THE SCENES of the follow-up to the smash-hit series Avatar: The Last Airbender! Each volume features hundreds of pieces of never-before-seen artwork created during the development of The Legend of Korra. With captions from creators Michael Dante DiMartino and Bryan Konietzko throughout, this is an intimate look inside the creative process that brought the mystical world of bending and a new generation of heroes to life!
nickelodeon
THE LEGEND OF KORRA™
THE ART OF THE ANIMATED SERIES
BOOK ONE: AIR
978-1-61655-168-1 | $34.99
BOOK TWO: SPIRITS
978-1-61655-462-0 | $34.99
BOOK THREE: CHANGE
978-1-61655-565-8 | $34.99
BOOK FOUR: BALANCE
978-1-61655-687-7 | $34.99
DARK HORSE BOOKS
AVAILABLE AT YOUR LOCAL COMICS SHOP | TO FIND A COMICS SHOP NEAR YOU, VISIT COMICSHOPLOCATOR.COM. For more information or to order direct: On the web: darkhorse.com
E-MAIL: mailorder@darkhorse.com · PHONE: 1-800-862-0052 Mon.–Fri. 9 AM to 5 PM Pacific Time.
The Legend of Korra© VIACOM INTERNATIONAL INC. All Rights Reserved. Dark Horse Books® and the Dark Horse logo are registered trademarks of Dark Horse Comics LLC. All rights reserved. (BL 6011)